To Sandy (illegible) april 26, '82
I hope you enjo(y) (illegible)
at the college. Best wishes,
Nathaniel Stampfer

THE

Solomon Goldman Lectures

Perspectives in Jewish Learning

Volume 3

Edited by
Nathaniel Stampfer

The Spertus College of Judaica Press
Chicago, Illinois

EDITOR'S PREFACE

The studies appearing in volume 3 of *The Solomon Goldman Lectures: Perspectives in Jewish Learning* were first delivered at Spertus College of Judaica as part of the annual lecture series the Solomon Goldman Lectures in Judaica. Spertus College and its press express their thanks to Mr. and Mrs. Sidney N. Shure of Chicago, whose consistent generosity has made possible both the Solomon Goldman Lectures and their publication. These volumes have made possible wide dissemination of the work of distinguished scholars in Judaic studies.

The lectures by eminent Judaic scholars and their publication are intended by Sidney and Rose Shure as a tribute to the memory of Rabbi Solomon Goldman, whose teaching, writings, and communal leadership represent an outstanding example of service and commitment.

Let it be noted that sustained sponsorship of the Solomon Goldman Lectures by the Shures is characterized by an exceptional dimension: Sidney and Rose Shure have not been remote, absentee benefactors but have added unfailing participation in all the lectures to their numerous other intellectual pursuits and artistic interests. *Tavo' alekhem berakha!*

The seven lectures contained herein focus on topics in the areas of Bible, Jewish history, Jewish thought, and Hebrew literature; hence, they represent most of the areas in Judaic studies. Thanks are extended to the seven distinguished contributors, who, following their appearances as Solomon Goldman lecturers, gave considerable time and effort to bring their lectures to publication.

Thanks are due Mr. Eugene Zucker, the copy editor, whose assistance enhanced the volume in many ways, and to the Office of Publications Services of the University of Illinois at Chicago Circle for bringing the volume to press.

November 1981

Contents

The Decalogue

Nahum M. Sarna

Brandeis University

I

The observation of Moses Maimonides (1135–1204 C.E.) that the Decalogue constitutes the very essence of religion[1] would probably be shared wholeheartedly by the votaries of all major religions. From earliest times this document has occupied a pivotal position in the Jewish religious consciousness.[2] Philo of Alexandria (born circa 20 B.C.E.) devoted a special treatise to the subject, in which he declared the Decalogue to be the summation (*Kephálaia*) of all the particular and special laws recorded in the Scriptures.[3] Rabbinic midrash similarly emphasized that the Decalogue contained the essential Torah from which all else is derived.[4] Little wonder that it achieved a position of such paramount importance that the daily morning service in the Second Temple once began with its recitation preceded by a blessing[5] and that it was at one time part of the contents of tefillin.[6]

It is taken for granted that the Decalogue comprises the minimal moral imperatives essential to the maintenance of an ordered and wholesome society, and that it is the great Jewish contribution to the world. But what was the state of affairs before Sinai? Was the world steeped in savagery and barbarism? The Bible itself assumes the existence of a moral code from the beginning of the appearance of human life on this planet.[7] Otherwise, how could Cain have been guilty of murder? For what "lawlessness" could God have brought the great flood, and for what "evil" would the inhabitants of Sodom and Gomorrah and their allied cities have been brought to account? The rabbinic notion of a "Noahide code," obligatory upon the human race, is itself a recognition of pre-Sinaitic norms of law and order.[8] Anyone with even an elementary knowledge of ancient history is aware that the people of Israel arrived very late on the world scene. By then the great civilizations of the Fertile Crescent had all passed their prime and were already heirs to ancient traditions and cultures. Obviously, these great civilizations could not have come about without a "social contract," a commitment to enforceable criteria of right and wrong that covered most of the principles enshrined in the Decalogue. This elementary presupposition is, in fact, well illustrated by the discovery of no less than six collections of laws from the ancient Near East, from the third millennium B.C.E. down.[9]

There are the laws of Ur-Nammu, king of the Sumerian city of Ur (circa 2050 B.C.E.); those of Bilalama, king of the Amorite city of Eshnunna (circa 1925 B.C.E.); the laws of Lipit-Ishtar, ruler of Isin (circa 1860 B.C.E.); the collection of Hammurabi of Babylon (circa 1700 B.C.E.); the Hittite code (circa fifteenth century B.C.E.); and the Assyrian laws from the city of Assur (circa 1350 B.C.E.). In addition to these, we have the wisdom and didactic literature of Egypt[10] and Mesopotamia,[11] which is replete with most of the injunctions found in the Decalogue, while magical texts, some of them from the Old Babylonian period (circa 1800 B.C.E.), often assume that sickness results from the violation of a taboo, and contain lists of wrongs committed, many of an ethical and moral nature.[12] Perhaps the most instructive text of all is the so-called *Book of the Dead* with its "negative confession."[13] This is a declaration or protestation of ignorance or innocence to be recited by the dead as a prior condition to entry into the next world. The negative formulation testifies to the reality of positive moral ideals, widely accepted as the indispensable imperatives of an ordered society. In the presence of Osiris and his court, convened in the "Hall of Two Truths," the dead man professed, among other items, "I have not committed evil among men, . . . I have not blasphemed a god, . . . I have not done violence to a poor man, . . . I have not killed, . . . I have not stolen, . . . I have not been covetous, . . . I have not robbed, . . . I have not told lies, . . . I have not committed adultery."

Clearly, the prohibitions of theft, murder, adultery, false witness, and so forth, were hardly novel at the time of the Exodus. Rather, they had long been accepted as the elementary standards of civilized, organized life. The fundamental question therefore arises: Wherein lay the uniqueness of Israel's contribution in giving the world the Decalogue?

II

One of the fundamental principles of rabbinic exegesis of the Bible is that the Scriptures employed contemporary forms and modes of speech in order to convey their message in an intelligible manner: "The Torah speaks in human language."[14] One of the major concerns of modern biblical scholars is to recover the "human language," the original life-setting of a scriptural passage, to discover why a text is expressed in the way it is and in the form it has assumed. Is there correlation between content and literary form? In other words, does an analysis of the typical structure of a biblical passage throw light on the context?

The only way such questions might be answered is by turning to the vast literature of the ancient Near East, which has preserved the "human language," the patterns of speech and the literary structures which were contemporaneous with the literary creativity of Israel or which were part of Israel's cultural baggage. Not always are the solutions forthcoming, but often they are, and in the case of the Decalogue comparative studies are particularly helpful.[15]

Now the term used in the Bible for the divine-Israelite encounter at Sinai is *berit*.[16] Hebrew makes no distinction in terminology between a covenant with God and a treaty drawn up between kings or between states or between two individuals.[17] All are termed *berit.* This fact provides a clue to the true significance of the Decalogue. The conventional Near Eastern treaty served as the conceptual model for the national experience at Sinai. In the ancient world of the Fertile Crescent, the covenant treaty was the recognized instrument by which desired relationships were effectuated and regulated. Many examples of such treaties have survived the ravages of time. They divide themselves roughly into three general groupings. There are the Hittite treaties from the second half of the second millennium B.C.E., Aramaic treaties from the ninth century B.C.E. from the Syro-Palestine sphere, and treaties from the Assyrian Empire from the ninth to the seventh centuries B.C.E.

It is the oldest group, the Hittite treaties, that are of particular interest in connection with the present topic. It has been noted that these conform to a more or less fixed basic literary pattern. In general, legal terminology and documentary patterns exhibit a remarkable tenacity and consistency in the ancient Near East. The training of scribes, of course, had a lot to do with it, as is proved by extant Mesopotamian formularies and vocabulary lists for scribes who specialized in legal phraseology.[18] Scribes and diplomats who drafted treaties in the Hittite Empire generally hewed closely to a basic prototypal structure covering six sections. First comes the "Preamble." The author of the treaty is identified by name, and his titles, attributes, and genealogy are listed. Next comes the "Historical Prologue," or introduction, which surveys the historical relationships between the contracting parties. In this section are detailed the past benefactions bestowed upon the vassal by the suzerain king, which are the basis for the vassal's present gratitude and future allegiance. Then follow, in turn, the "Stipulations," which are the core of the treaty; the call for the "Deposition" of a copy of the treaty in the vassal's sanctuary, with provision for its periodic public reading; and a long list of gods who act as "Witnesses" to the terms of the document. Finally, the "Curses and Blessings" complete the covenant, the former describing the dire consequences of the vassal's infraction of the treaty terms, the latter pointing to the beneficial results of faithful adherence to them.[19]

III

Turning now to the Covenant at Sinai, one may detect at once the striking similarities between it and the Hittite treaty forms just described. The Decalogue opens with a preamble identifying the author of the Covenant: "I am the Lord your God."[20] Then comes the historical prologue, a retrospect of the benefactions that God has wrought for Israel: "who brought you out of the land of Egypt, the house of bondage."[21] This is the overriding, pivotal event, the dominant theme in Israelite history that cemented the relations between God and Israel, and that remained the cause for Israel's eternal gratitude and the basis of the obligations it owed Him. The third section, the "Thou shalt" and "Thou shalt not," comprises

3

the stipulations,[22] the principles on which the future relations of Israel to God are to be based. The other three elements that characterize the Hittite treaties are not included in the Decalogue itself, but they are present elsewhere in the account of the Sinaitic revelation. A copy of the Covenant is required to be deposited in the sanctuary,[23] and provision is made for the periodic public reading of the text.[24] Of course, there is no room for gods as witnesses in Israel's monotheistic religion, but their place is taken by "heaven and earth,"[25] or by memorial stones,[26] and the curses and blessings—in reverse order—are very much alive in the great "Reproofs," or *Tokhahot*.[27]

IV

What significance attaches to the fact that the ancient Near Eastern treaty pattern became the model for the expression of the division of the divine-human encounter at Sinai? First and foremost it must be stressed with every emphasis at one's command that in using the term *berit*, "Covenant," the Bible is not resorting to a mere figure of speech, but is describing a living reality, an actual legal circumstance, nothing less than the assertion of an actual, eternally binding pact between God and His people.[28] Just as the ancient treaties served to regularize and control relationships between one individual and another and between one state and another, so the Covenant at Sinai aimed to delineate the proper relationships between God and Israel. But there is also one fundamental difference. The Near Eastern treaties are political documents that usually affect only the foreign policies of states. They do not infringe upon internal affairs except insofar as these impinge upon the interests of the suzerain state. The Sinai Covenant, on the other hand, projects a revolutionary expansion of the original concept, first by including each and every aspect of life within the treaty stipulations, and then by making God and an entire people the parties to the Covenant. These two features of the biblical exemplar are absolutely unique. There is no parallel in history for such concepts, no analogy to Israel's claim to have undergone a national religious experience, no conceptual prototype for that claim.

No less revolutionary than the innovations themselves are the consequences that flow from them. The entire nation of Israel is conceived as being a corporate entity, a "psychic totality." The obligation to keep the law is national, societal, and communal. Evil is a breach of the Covenant that undermines society. The welfare of society, the integrity of its fabric, is contingent upon the observance of the law.[29] No wonder that the conventional treaty provision requiring periodic public reading of the treaty's stipulations was expanded in Israel and transformed into a wholly new dimension—the obligation, oft-repeated, to disseminate the law among the masses, the universal duty of continuous self-education.[30]

In the ancient Near East the opposite was the case. Hammurabi, it is true, wrote the laws—so he said—so that a plaintiff or defendant might know what they were.[31] But this was largely a fiction, since mass illiteracy was the rule, and interest in the law was aroused only after the inception of a case, and was restricted to the details of the particular paragraph of the code that applied in the circumstances. More in common with the spirit of Mesopotamian society was the injunction forbidding the dissemination of the details of the temple service for the New Year festival.[32] One is reminded of the fact that until Draco (circa 621 B.C.E.) codified the laws of Athens, these remained the exclusive knowledge of the nobility, and their publication among the masses was forbidden. Diametrically opposed to such a notion is the biblical outlook. In Judaism the mass dissemination of the law in all its details is a major priority. The reason is obvious. Law is not simply an intellectual exercise, but a moral discipline through whose instrumentality the entire society is shaped.

V

A further crucial distinction between the Decalogue and ancient Near Eastern codes lies in the source and sanction of law. No biblical law is ever attributed to Moses himself or to any prophet personally. The narratives know nothing of a lawgiver-sage or a lawgiver-king. The great empire builders and organizers, David and Solomon, have no connection with law codes. The great reformers Jehoshaphat,[33] Hezekiah,[34] and Josiah[35] reorganize the judiciary and the cult, but they do so only to implement the ancient law of God. They make no claim to innovation. The only name exclusively connected with law is that of Moses, and he is a prophet who mediates the divine communication to Israel.

This picture is in striking contrast to the situation in the ancient world, where the legislators are kings, princes, and sages. The king and the state constitute the source of law, its sanction, and the authority behind it.[36] It is perfectly true that the polytheistic gods themselves did not behave according to moral norms, but they did, nevertheless, desire that mankind be in possession of just laws. They wanted the king to establish justice in the land. Some gods, such as Shamash, the sun-god, were looked upon as the custodians of justice and equity. Thus, Hammurabi invokes the gods in the prologue to his laws, and the stela on which they are inscribed is decorated with a relief depicting Shamash presiding over their promulgation.[37] The text, however, leaves no doubt that Hammurabi ascribes the laws to himself: "I established law and justice in the language of the land."[38] "The laws of justice which Hammurabi, the efficient king, set up."[39] "I am the king who is preeminent among the kings; my words are choice; my ability has no equal. By the order of Shamash, the great judge of heaven and earth, may my justice prevail in the land; by the word of Marduk, my lord, may my statutes have no one to rescind them."[40] It is very much Hammurabi who is the author of the laws, not the gods. The role of the god in law is to serve as the source of wisdom, as the one who implants in man the faculty of discernment and truth and the perception of justice. This is what enables kings to make righteous laws. But the actual origin and source of law lie in human wisdom, not in the revealed will of the gods. The biblical claim that the law, in fact, constitutes the revealed will of God remains unparalleled.

VI

There is no biblical tradition to indicate how the Decalogue was distributed over the tablets of stone.[41] The Pentateuch invariably refers to tablets, in the plural,[42] and usually mentions two specifically,[43] but what was written on each is not clarified. The Tannaitic midrash on Exodus—the Mekhilta—assumes that there were five on each tablet,[44] and Jewish art has fossilized this interpretation. In the Talmud of Palestine, however, another tradition is evident, to the effect that the Ten Commandments were written *in toto* on each stone separately.[45] Both traditions reflect an acute perception of the essential nature of Torah legislation, namely, that the covenant idea suffuses every aspect of life.

The Decalogue, indeed, falls more or less naturally into two divisions. The first four "Words" indubitably relate to the divine-human sphere; the last five clearly govern interpersonal relationships; and the fifth acts as a kind of bridge between the two parts, for the Bible uses the same vocabulary for revering parents as for revering God.

This balance between what we would call the "religious" and the "social" is well illustrated by the opening and closing words: "God . . . fellowman." Each of the first five declarations contains the phrase "the Lord your God," which does not appear in the last five. The "religious" demands precede the "sociomoral" because only a sense of responsibility to God provides the ultimate guarantee of the observance of our duties toward our fellow beings;[46] conversely, professed belief in God, and the observance of the outward forms of religious expression, are well-nigh worthless unless they profoundly affect human relationships. This interweaving of the spiritual, the cultic, the moral, and the legal, this lack of differentiation between "religious" matters, matters of interpersonal relationships, and matters of social and sexual morality—this is the quintessential differentiating characteristic of biblical law. All other systems in the ancient world display an atomistic approach to life. Civil obligations belong to the domain of law, moral demands to the domain of wisdom literature, cultic responsibilities to the domain of priestly handbooks. Law is strictly secular in content. In Israel, however, life is treated holistically. It is not compartmentalized. Crime is also sin. An offense against sexual morality, against business morality, against social morality, is simultaneously a "religious" offense because one and all they are infractions of the divine will.

VII

It will surely have been noted that the Decalogue is distinguished by the total absence of specific individual penalties for the violation of the injunctions and prohibitions. We find only "Thou shalt" or "Thou shalt not." These apodictic formulations have no definitions, no limitations, no punishments—they are unqualified, absolute declarations.[47] This is no coincidence. The phenomenon goes to the very heart of the meaning and significance of the Decalogue.

What the apodictic formulation asserts is that there are certain God-given values and behavioral norms which are absolute and not self-originating; morality is the expression of the divine will, and the motivation for observing the law is not fear of punishment but the desire to conform to the will of God. The Decalogue is a self-enforcing code that appeals to the conscience, the spiritual discipline, and the moral fiber of the individual, not to the threat of penalty that can be imposed by the external coercive power of the state. Of course, we do not live in a utopian society, and, as the Mishnah expresses it, "were it not for the fear of government, people would devour each other alive."[48] So elsewhere in the Torah the casuistic pattern of law with its specific penalties is the general rule.

The Decalogue is obviously not meant to provide an alternative to the coercive power of the state. But the dismal record of the modern state in providing for its citizens' quality of life suggests that without the value system of the Decalogue, society is unlikely to make much progress in solving its chronic ills.

NOTES

1. *Commentary to Mishnah*, Tamid 5:1.

2. The Decalogical tradition is already evident in biblical literature; cf. Jer. 7:9; Hos. 4:2, 12:10; 13:4; Ps. 81:10.

3. *De Decalogo, Philo Judaeus*, Loeb Classical Library, trans. F. H. Colson (London-Cambridge, 1937), 7:82–83, sec. 154.

4. Canticles Rabba 5:12; cf. Numbers Rabba 13:15. For an exhaustive list of the specific laws derived from each of the Ten Commandments, see *Ozar Yisrael*, ed. J. D. Eisenstein (New York, 1951), 8:154–68.

5. Mishnah Tamid 5:1; cf. B. Berakhot 11b–12a; P. Berakhot 1:8 (3c). On this subject, see L. Blau, "Origine et histoire de la lecture du schema," *Revue des Études Juives* 31 (1895): 179–201; V. Aptowitzer, "L'Usage de la lecture quotidienne du Décalogue à la synagogue et l'explication de Mathieu 19:16–19 et 22:35–40," *Revue des Études Juives* 88 (1929): 167–70; and G. Vermes, "The Decalogue and the Minim," *In Memoriam: Paul Kahle*, ed. M. Black and G. Fohrer (Berlin, 1968), pp. 232–40.

6. Mishnah Sanhedrin 11:3 mentions the possibility of five passages in the tefillin, but without specifying the Decalogue. *Sifre Deuteronomy*, ed. M. Friedmann (Vienna, 1864), 74b, sec. 35, makes clear that this is the issue. The church father Jerome (340–420 C.E.) reports that he actually saw tefillin containing the Decalogue. On this entire subject, see J. Mann, "Changes in the Divine Service of the Synagogue due to Religious Persecutions," *Hebrew Union College Annual* 4 (1927): 241–310. The finding of such tefillin at Qumran has fully vindicated Mann's position; see Y. Yadin, *Tefillin from Qumran (XQ Phyl. 1–4)* (Jerusalem, 1969), especially pp. 27–29, 34 f., 40.

7. Y. Kaufmann, *Toledoth HaEmunah HaYisreelith* (Tel-Aviv, 1952–56), has repeatedly made this point; cf. 1:185, 2:76 f.

8. There is no rabbinic unanimity as to the content of the "Noahide commandments." The list that enjoys the widest consensus is as follows: the prohibition of idolatry, blasphemy, bloodshed, incest, and robbery; the injunction to establish courts of law; and the proscription of eating from the body of a

living animal (Tosefta Abodah Zarah 9[8]:4; B. Sanhedrin 56a; Maimonides, *Yad Ḥazakah,* Melakhim 9:1). On Maimonides' view, see Marvin Fox, *Diné Israel* (Tel Aviv University, 1972), 3:v–xxxvi.

9. J. B. Pritchard, *Ancient Near Eastern Texts Relating to the Old Testament* (hereinafter referred to as ANET), 2d ed. (Princeton, 1955), pp. 159–98; and *Supplementary Texts* (Princeton, 1969), p. 528.

10. ANET, pp. 412–25.

11. ANET, pp. 425–30; and W. G. Lambert, *Babylonian Wisdom Literature* (Oxford, 1960).

12. The reference is to the so-called atonement magic of the Shurpu series; see S. H. Hooke, *Babylonian and Assyrian Religion* (London, 1962), p. 96 f.

13. E. Wallis Budge, *The Book of the Dead,* reprint (New York, 1960), p. 568 ff.; *The Egyptian Book of the Dead,* trans. Th. G. Allen (Chicago, 1974), pp. 97–99; and ANET, p. 34 ff.

14. Cf. B. Berakhoth 31b; Yebamoth 71a; Kethuboth 67b.

15. S. Goldman, *The Ten Commandments,* ed. Maurice Samuel (Chicago, 1956); J. J. Stamm and M. E. Andrew, *The Ten Commandments in Recent Research* (Naperville, Ill., 1967); and E. Nielsen, *The Ten Commandments in New Perspective* (Naperville, Ill., 1968).

16. Exod. 34:10, 27; Deut. 5:2.

17. E.g., Gen. 14:3; 21:27, 32; and 31:44.

18. Cf. the Old Babylonian compendium called *ana ittishu,* published by B. Landsberger, *Materialien zum sumerischen Lexikon,* vol. 1 (Rome, 1937).

19. G. E. Mendenhall, *Law and Covenant in Israel and the Ancient Near East* (Pittsburgh, 1955), has thoroughly examined the relevant material. See also K. Baltzer, *The Covenant Formulary* (Oxford, 1971); D. J. McCarthy, *Treaty and Covenant* (Rome, 1963); D. R. Hillers, *Covenant: The History of A Biblical Idea* (Baltimore, 1969); K. A. Kitchen, *Ancient Orient and Old Testament* (Chicago, 1973), pp. 90–102; and B. Uffenheimer, *HaNebuah HaQedumah BeYisrael* (Jerusalem, 1973), pp. 70–94.

20. Exod 20:2; Deut. 5:6. This same self-identifying, introductory form of address is characteristic of Canaanite-Phoenician royal proclamations. So in those of Mesha of Moab (ANET, p. 320), Yehawmilk of Byblos (ANET, p. 502), Kilamuwa of Ya'udi (Sam'al; ANET, p. 500), Zakir of Hamath and Lu'ath (ANET, p. 501), Azitawadda of Adana (ANET, p. 499), and Bar-Rakab of Ya'udi (ANET, p. 501).

21. Exod. 20:2; Deut. 5:6.

22. Exod. 20:3–17; Deut. 5:7–18. Maimonides, *Sefer HaMadda'* 1:6, interpreted verse 2, "I am the LORD your God," to be a positive commandment of belief in one God, and the traditional Jewish order lists this as the first commandment. It should be pointed out that the biblical texts (Exod. 34:28; Deut. 4:3, 10:6) speak of "ten words/declarations" (Hebrew *'aseret ha-debarim.* The postbiblical title *'aseret ha-dibbrot* derives from a singular *dibber* (Jer. 5:13), not *dibbrah.* For the feminine plural form of a masculine singular, cf. *kissé–kisseot, maqqel–maqqlot.*

23. Exod. 25:16; Deut. 10:5, 31:9, 24–26; cf. 1 Kings 8:9 = 2 Chron. 5:10.

24. Deut. 31:10–13.

25. Deut. 4:26, 30:19, 32:1.

26. Exod. 24:4; cf. Josh. 24:27.

27. Lev., chap. 26; Deut., chap. 28; cf. Josh. 24:19–20.

28. W. Eichrodt, *Theology of the Old Testament,* vol. 1 (Philadelphia, 1961), has emphasized this point.

29. Cf. Lev. 18:24–30, 26:3–13; Deut. 11:13–15, 22–32; 28:1–14.

30. Cf. Exod. 21:1; Deut. 31:1, 10–13; Neh. 8:1–8.

31. ANET, p. 178; C. H. rev., xxv:3–19.

32. ANET, p. 331; cf. p. 334.

33. 2 Chron. 19:5–11, on which see W. F. Albright, "The Judicial Reform of Jehoshaphat," in *Alexander Marx Jubilee Volume,* ed. Saul Lieberman (New York, 1950), pp. 61–82.

34. 2 Chron., chaps. 29–31.

35. 2 Kings, chaps. 22–23; 2 Chron., chaps. 34–35.

36. This point has been well made by Kaufmann, *Toledoth,* 2:587 f.

37. J. B. Pritchard, *The Ancient Near East in Pictures* (Princeton, 1954), #515.

38. ANET, p. 165, prologue, v, 20.

39. ANET, p. 177, epilogue, reverse, xxiv, 1.

40. ANET, p. 178, epilogue, reverse, xxiv, 80.

41. On this subject, see Sh. HaKohen Weingarten, " 'Aséret ha-dibbrot vehaluqatan," *Beth Mikra* 59 (1974): 549–71; and Th. Radai, " 'Od 'al 'aséret ha-dibbrot ve-haluqatan," *Beth Mikra* 62 (1975): 404 f.

42. Exod. 24:12; 32:16, 19; 34:28; Deut. 9:9; 10:2, 4, 5.

43. Exod. 31:18; 32:15; 34:4, 29; Deut. 4:13; 5:19; 9:9–11, 15,17; 10:1, 3; 1 Kings 9:8 = 2 Chron. 5:10.

44. J. Z. Lauterbach, *Mekhilta de-Rabbi Ishmael* (Philadelphia, 1949), 2:262.

45. P. Sheqalim 6:1.

46. This is the implication of Lev. 19:18.

47. On apodictic and casuistic law, see Kitchen, *Ancient Orient,* p. 147 f.

48. Mishnah Abot 3:2.

Law and Ethics in Maimonides' Theology

David Novak

Old Dominion University

Solomon Goldman was profoundly interested in Maimonides, and in 1936 he published a study of Maimonides' thought, *The Jew and The Universe,* as his contribution to the celebration of the 800th anniversary of Maimonides' birth in 1135. In the conclusion to this work Dr. Goldman noted the centrality of the Law in Maimonides' thought.

> Judaism, Maimonides guessed, was a living entity only because and insofar as its Law lives
> . . . and, therefore, [he] expended his major efforts not in primary philosophy but on the
> exposition, codification and application of the Law, not the theoretic law of some imaginary
> Republic but the laws affecting the Jew's daily life, making for the continuity of the Jewish
> people, for the preservation and enhancing of specific Jewish values.[1]

Surely Dr. Goldman was correct if we view the quantity of Maimonides' literary output. Most of it was devoted to questions of Jewish law, of Halakhah. However, Dr. Goldman also indicated that Maimonides was concerned with the deeper philosophic meaning of the Law as well as with its more immediate normative meanings.[2] Therefore, I feel correct in interpreting the above-quoted passage to indicate that *even* Maimonides' interest in "primary philosophy," namely metaphysics, was essentially connected with his interest in the Law. In this paper I shall try to show how Maimonides constituted this essential connection between law and metaphysics. An explanation of the terms used in the title of the paper—*law, ethics, theology*—should prove helpful in introducing the main question to be discussed.

For Maimonides, metaphysics is concerned primarily with God. Thus, metaphysics is "theology" in the original Greek meaning of that term—*theos legein,* precisely what we call today "God-talk."[3] "The Law" consists of normative prescriptions governing all aspects of human action. "Ethics" might be defined as the theory of the legal or moral prescriptions governing human action. Therefore, our question is: How does the relation between the prescription of action and its theory find its grounding in a philosophic concern with God?

The Locus Classicus of Maimonides' Philosophy of Law

Jewish law, as presented in the classical rabbinic sources, can be divided into two general categories. The first category, the larger one, deals with the obligations of the Jewish people, beginning with the 613 commandments of the written Torah. The second category, the smaller one, deals with the obligations of the Gentiles, the so-called seven commandments of the sons of Noah.

Maimonides posits a relation between Noahide law and Torah law. He sees a process of revelation beginning with Adam and concluding with Moses, "by means of whom the Torah was completed" *(v'nishlemah Torah 'al yado)*.[4] Now this "completion" does not refer merely to the numerical completion of the commandments of the Torah, beginning with 7 and culminating with 613. (Indeed, the 7 Noahide commandments per se are not counted as part of the 613 commandments of the Mosaic Torah.)[5] For Maimonides, who is so prone to using Aristotelian concepts, "completion" means that the full Torah can be seen *potentially* in Noahide law.[6] Therefore, Maimonides' treatment of Torah law in general has its simplest application in his understanding of Noahide law. Noahide law and Torah law are thus members of the same genus—divine law—differing only in that the latter is a more complex development of the former. This is where we should begin to look for the answer to our question about law and ethics and their grounding in Maimonides' metaphysics, his theology.

Regarding the source of Gentile obligation, Maimonides writes,

> Concerning six things was the first man commanded [*nitzaveh*]. . . . Even though [*af 'al pi*] they are all traditional [*kabbalah*], coming from Moses our master to our hands, and reason inclines to them [*vehada' at noteh lahen*], from Scripture it is generally evident [*mikhlal*] that he was so commanded concerning them. The prohibition of eating a limb torn from a living animal [*eber min hahai*] was added for Noah.[7]

Thus there are three possible sources for Noahide law: (1) Mosaic tradition, (2) rational inclination,[8] and (3) general divine revelation in Scripture. Maimonides opts for the third source. In so doing, however, he does not eliminate the other two as contradicting this true source. Indeed, he mentions that in addition to being divinely revealed, these laws are *also* traditional and rational.

In the immediately preceding section of the *Mishneh Torah*, Maimonides answers the question of how the Noahide laws are known.

> Any Gentile who does not accept the commandments for which the Noahides were commanded: we are to execute him if he is under our political control [*yeshno tahat yadeynu*]. . . . whoever accepts the seven commandments, being obliged [*nizhar*] to do them . . . because [*mipnay*] God commanded them in the Torah and made us aware through Moses our master that the Noahides were previously [*me' kodem*] commanded concerning them. . . . he did them because of rational conclusion.[9]

Here again there are three possibilities: (1) Noahide law is known because it is promulgated by Jewish authorities to Gentiles living under their political rule; (2) Noahide law is known because of the acceptance by the Gentiles of divine revelation to the Jews; and (3) Noahide law is known because it is rationally convincing. Maimonides opts for the second possibility as alone being fully adequate as the ultimate source of Noahide law. Thus only the person who consciously affirms this true source of Noahide law qualifies as "one of the saints of the nations of the world" (*mehasiday umot ha'olam*) and is assured of a "portion in the world to come" (*'olam haba*). However, just as revelation as the source of the law did not eliminate either Mosaic tradition or reason, so the conscious acceptance of revelation does not eliminate acceptance based on compliance with Jewish political rule or acceptance based on rational conclusions.[9]

Although Maimonides states that those who accept the Noahide laws because of rational conclusion alone are not participants in the transcendent realm of the world to come, he does not state that they have failed to fulfill the *legal* requirements of these laws. In other words, a person who fails to regard these laws as divine commandments is not thereby a transgressor. Fulfillment of the Noahide laws on the positive legal level merely implies a recognition of their legal authority, and however inadequate such an approach may be from a metaphysical standpoint, it is legally acceptable.[10] Moreover, this approach does not contradict the metaphysical foundation of the law as long as it does not claim to be wholly adequate, which it is not. Furthermore, the approach is consistent with the rabbinic view that religious intention (*kavvanah*) is not a legal prerequisite for those commandments which involve external action alone.[11] None of the Noahide laws specifically prescribes an inner attitude. All concern outward behavior.

The Noahide laws involve three assertions: (1) they were promulgated by God to the sons of Noah, as described by Scripture; (2) they are obligatory for all mankind; and (3) they enable one to achieve the bliss of the world to come. Now the third assertion is contingent on the first; that is, *if* one believes God commanded these laws to the sons of Noah, *then* one is assured of heavenly bliss.[12] However, the second assertion can stand alone, independent of either the first or the third. In other words, Maimonides acknowledges the possibility—though not the desirability—of rational discovery of the Noahide laws even without regard for their transcendent origins or consequences. Legally they stand alone. Rational discovery of the Noahide laws, however, does not preclude a recognition of their transcendent origins or consequences. Only metaphysically is the specific rationality of the Noahide laws an insufficient explanation of their full meaning for man. Furthermore, we shall see that Maimonides does not regard "rational conclusion" (*hekhre'a hada'at*), or what we might today call "induction," to be the only or even the highest form of ratiocination.[13] Thus the insufficiency of rational conclusion might very well be that it insufficiently *reasons* about the deeper meaning of the Noahide laws. Maimonides is not making reason and revelation mutually exclusive; rather, he is rejecting a certain type of nonmetaphysical reasoning as being too superficial to grasp the rational meaning of the divine law.

Concerning the relation between proper and improper motivation in the observance of the law, the Talmud much earlier noted,

> Let a man always engage in the study of the Torah and the performance of the commandments even for ulterior motives [*shelo lishmah*], because even from out of [*mitokh*] such motives he will indeed come to do them for their own sake [*lishmah*].[14]

Since, then, Maimonides does not present reason and revealed law as being mutually exclusive, we will have to see how he constitutes the relation between them. This will require looking at other passages from the *Mishneh Torah;* at an important, often ignored, responsum of Maimonides; and, especially, at the *Guide of the Perplexed,* which Maimonides himself regarded as the more philosophic treatment of many of the questions suggested by Halakhah and Aggadah, questions with which he himself dealt so expertly in his earlier works.[15]

Since Maimonides designates Noahide law (and *a fortiori* the law of the Torah) as divine law, we must now examine how he defines divine law and how he distinguishes it from human law.

Divine Law: Rational and Revealed

Law is categorized in terms of its source and its goal, namely, the origin of its promulgation and the end of its legislation.[16]

The source of the divine law for Maimonides, as we have already seen from the *Mishneh Torah,* is the revealed will of God. In the *Guide* he is more specific about what he means by revelation. He defines prophecy, the presupposition of the revelation of the Torah, as follows:

> Know that the true reality and quiddity [*mahutah*] of prophecy consist in its being an overflow [*shefa'*] overflowing from God . . . through the intermediation of the active intellect [*bemtza'ut hasekhel hapo'el*], toward the rational faculty [*koah hadibbry*] in the first place and thereafter toward the imaginative faculty [*koah hamedameh*]. This is the highest degree of man and the ultimate term of perfection [*takhlit hashelemut*] that can exist for his species.[17]

For Maimonides the "rational faculty" is concerned with the unchanging objects of intellection (*muskalot*), namely, the heavenly bodies and the principles of metaphysics. Judgments in this area are in terms of "true and false" (*emet v'sheker*). The "imaginative faculty," on the other hand, is concerned with the changing political issues of human society (*mefursamot*), namely, the opinions and values by which human beings live together. Judgments in this area are in terms of "good and bad" (*tob v'ra*).[18] However, if the prophet is a person who combines intellectual and political excellence to the highest extent humanly possible,[19] then there must be a relation between intellectual and political reality to which the combined excellence of the prophet corresponds.

Earlier, Maimonides designated as *clear and manifest* "primary intelligibles" (*muskalim rishonim*) and "things perceived by the senses" (*murgashim*).[20] Among the latter he includes "the existence of man's ability to act" (*hayyekholet l'adam*). Now the difference between primary intelligibles and sensibles, such as motion, is that the former are abstract and the latter concrete. However, there is a relation between them over and above their being "clear and manifest." This relation is that the abstraction of intelligible forms from concrete particulars presupposes an intimate awareness of sensibles. For it is reflection on the paradoxes of the senses, especially the paradox of motion, which stimulates the intellect to discover such abstract concepts as causality.[21] Thus awareness of the objects of sense is a noetic means to knowledge of the intelligibles to which they point. The existence of man's ability to act—that is, human freedom—which Maimonides designates as the presupposition of all law, is, like motion, a primary sensible.[22]

Now man's ability to act can never be denied if the concept of law as *commandment* is to be valid. Maimonides makes this point in many places, but most lucidly, I think, in his discussion of the phenomenon of repentance (*teshubah*) in the *Mishneh Torah*.

> If God were to decree that man is to be righteous or wicked, . . . like the view the astrologers [*hobray hashamayim*] invent from their own minds, how could He command [*metzaveh*] us by means of prophets "do this" and "do not do that" . . . ? what role [*makom*] would there be for the entire Torah?[23]

He goes on to say that God included human freedom in the created order just as He included all other natural phenomena. God does not change the general natural structure of the created universe.[24] Even miracles are only particularly unusual occurrences. But they too are part of the natural order of creation.[25]

Nevertheless, Maimonides' understanding of the metaphysical meaning of human freedom can be misunderstood if we read into it modern views which see freedom as a value. For Maimonides, freedom is a fact, not a value; that is, it is something which man has more in common with animals than with angels.[26] It is not meant to be an object of human aspiration, but an element of necessity in the human condition. Thus the denial of human freedom would imply that, like the heavenly bodies, man has achieved his rational perfection. Experience surely indicates that this is not the case. The denial of human freedom is, then, an overestimation rather than an underestimation of the human condition. Note how Maimonides describes it.

> It is a fundamental principle of the Law of Moses our master . . . that man has an absolute ability to act [*ba'al hayyekholet gemurah*]; I mean to say that in virtue of his nature, his choice [*ubehirato*], and his will [*ubirtzono*], he may do everything that is within the capacity of man to do. . . . Similarly [*v'khen*], all the species of animals move in virtue of their own will.[27]

Thus man's distinction from the animals, in terms of his ability to act, is one of degree rather than kind. Ibn Shem Tob, the fifteenth century commentator on the *Guide,* points out that "choice" is a more "rational" (*sikhlit*) thing than mere "will" (*ratzon*) and that Maimonides uses it in regard to man but not in regard to animals.[28] Nevertheless, the underlying general similarity is far greater than this specific difference. Desire, which determines locomotion, is shared by man with other sublunar beings. Desire is attracted by what it perceives as good and repulsed by what it perceives as bad.[29] Originally, man, like the heavenly beings, was beyond these mundane considerations, concerned only with matters of truth and falsehood. His "fall" in the Garden of Eden removed him from this pristine level.[30] Since then, his task has been to ground the world of desire (*mefursamot*) in the world of intelligibility (*muskalot*). Thus human freedom is man's awareness of his incomplete status in this world.

Like other sensibles, human freedom must be explained in terms of its proper end. Just as motion can only be explained in terms of its direction, so man's ability to act can only be explained in terms of its ultimate goal. For Maimonides, the ultimate destination of all human action is God's direct presence. God's knowability as the cosmic end (*telos*) is a primary intelligible.[31] Therefore, the relation between sensibles (including human action) and intelligibles is teleological: the latter are the ultimate ends of the former.

The fact that the ultimate end of human action exists prior to man's attainment of it means that it is *discovered,* not constructed. Thus God, through the active intellect, has to make this ultimate knowledge move from a state of potentiality to one of actuality in the human mind. For Maimonides follows Aristotle in assuming that nothing can move from a potential to an actual state without an external efficient cause.[32] This is why the knowability of the divine law requires revelation to a prophet. The Neoplatonic motif of "overflowing" or "emanation" expresses the relation between the intelligible realm and the sensible realm viewed from the perspective of the intelligible realm.[33] It is from this vantage point that the source of revelation is considered to be the will of God.

For Maimonides, however, it is always preferable to view creation from the perspective of divine wisdom. When we know the proper end of any created entity—and the Torah is a created entity—we can then speak of divine wisdom.[34] To insist on divine volition to the exclusion of immanent ends is to eliminate intelligibility from creation. Such a point of view reduces the divine will to divine caprice. Ultimately, however, there is wisdom in everything that God does. The fact that we are unable to discover that wisdom in *everything* does not mean that we are unable to discover it in *anything*.[35] As regards the commandments of the Torah, Maimonides emphasizes that even though we can discern a general reason for every commandment, we do not know the reasons for the particulars of many commandments. We can see the divine wisdom in the *essential* structure of the Torah and its institutions.[36] We are frequently unable, however, to detect the divine wisdom in the *existential* details. On such occasions we defer to the divine will.[37] In essence, the divine will and the divine wisdom are the same, differing only in their manifestations.[38]

The Correlation between Law and Metaphysics

The correlation between law and metaphysics begins with the earliest manifestation of law in the political community.

Viewed in itself, the political arena seems to be turbulent and disordered, nothing more than the scene of struggle, ambition, greed, and, ofttimes, danger. However, the very fact that man is greatly disappointed in this turbulence and disorder indicates that he has an inkling of something more ordered, something which contradicts the prima facie divisiveness of political life. Maimonides describes this tension as follows:

> It has been explained with utmost clarity that man is political by nature [*medini beteba'*] and that it is his nature to live in a society. . . . Because of the manifold composition of this species, . . . there are many differences between the individuals belonging to it. . . . the nature of the human species requires that there be those differences among the individuals belonging to it. . . . in addition, society is a necessity for this nature [*el hakibbutz tzorekh hakorhi*].[39]

Maimonides then suggests that the political nature of man, which manifests itself as a striving for political unity, leads to the emergence of a leader who attempts to narrow the differences among men by introducing laws, uniform rules of conduct that apply equally to all men and thus unite them all in one political community.[40] If a leader's sole aim is to bring about political cohesiveness without regard for the discovery of truth, with which the rational faculty is concerned, then the leader is simply an inventive personality and laws are man-made (*nimusim*).[41] In other words, the intent of the laws indicates their source.

> If, on the other hand, you find a Law all of whose ordinances are due to attention being paid . . . to the soundness of the circumstances pertaining to the body and also to the soundness of belief—a Law that takes pains to inculcate correct opinions with regard to God . . . and that desires to make man wise, to give him understanding, and to awaken his attention, so that he should know the whole of that which exists in its true form [*'al tekhunat ha-emet*]— you must know that this guidance [*z'ot ha'hanhagah*] comes from Him . . . and that this Law is divine [*Elohit*].[42]

The political nature of man aspires to perpetual unity (*hok ehad tamid*) and order (*seder*), ideals which are ultimately grounded in the intelligible realm. The prophet sees this essential connection, and he thereby sees the solution to society's dilemma in the encouragement of and preparation for "speculative matters" (*'inyanim iyyuniim*), whose apex is the true knowledge of God.[43] The inventive political leader, on the other hand, only sees prudent solutions to immediate political problems. He is not interested in the metaphysical foundation of law. However, and this is crucial, Maimonides does not view this type of limited insight as immoral but only as metaphysically unsatisfying. The inventive political leader, it seems to me, is the type of person whom Maimonides described in the *Mishneh Torah* as observing Noahide law because of "rational conclusion" (*hekhre'a hada'at*). Such rational conclusion, oblivious to the divine source of the law and the divine end of the law, is a sort of prudence. It is the type of thinking we would probably now term "utilitarian."

The initial motivation of any political leader, be he statesman or prophet, is to bring unity out of diversity, harmony out of chaos. Therefore, the legislation of any political leader is given in universal norms. From the point of view of individuals, law seems inherently inadequate because it cannot possibly address itself to their particular differences. However, these very differences, with their resultant strife and misery, are the source of the fundamental problems of the human condition. Consequently, the universality is not a weakness of law but its greatest strength.

> The Law does not pay attention to the isolated. The Law was not given with a view to things that are rare. . . . For the Law is a divine thing ['inyan Elohi]; and it is your business to reflect on the natural things [ha'inyanim hatib'iyim] in which the general utility [hatoelet hakollelet], which is included in them, nonetheless produces damages to individuals [n'zakim p'ratim].[44]

Now the question arises, How can the divine, immutable Torah produce damaging results for some individuals?[45] The answer seems to be that this depends on how individuals participate in the community constituted by the divine law. If their participation is basically a tacit contract, in which they give up *unlimited* freedom for political protection, that is, society's sanction to pursue *limited* individual freedoms, then it is very likely that in some cases this will be a bad bargain. In other words, some individuals will give away more than they will get back. If, on the other hand, social participation is motivated by a desire to imitate nature, to participate in a realm of greater unity and order, then the sacrifice of unlimited human prerogatives cannot ultimately harm anyone who has risen to this level of wisdom. For understanding the true ends of human society enables one to experience divine providence (*hashgahah*), which functions on the specific rather than the individual level.[46] When one becomes a "species being,"[47] that is, when one lives within the perspective of proper human teleology, he participates in a realm which is not only ideal but which to a certain extent has become real for him. Herein lies the difference between the political leadership of an ordinary statesman and that of a prophet. The ordinary statesman understands only the prudential value of political unity and order. He does not understand their metaphysical grounding, their teleological meaning. The prophet, conversely, transcends the statesman in his vision of this metaphysical grounding of ethics.[48] The difference in perspective is between "intellection" (*'iyyun*) and "estimation" (*hekhre'a hada'at*).[49] Therefore, it seems to me that Maimonides bases his refusal to include among the Gentile saints who merit the world to come those who practice the Noahide laws because of rational conviction alone upon a distinction between prudential reasoning, which deals only with human matters (*nomos*), and metaphysical reasoning, which deals with divine matters. Such prudential reasoning seems to refer to the "bringer of the nomos" (*meni'a hanimus*), whom Maimonides contrasts with the prophet.[50]

Moral Wisdom

By understanding the important distinction between the prophet and the statesman, we can perhaps solve a crucial textual problem in the statement of Maimonides' philosophy of law in the *Mishneh Torah*, which we examined earlier.

It will be recalled that Maimonides stipulates that only Gentiles who accept the

Noahide law as revealed qualify as "saints" (*hasidim*) who merit heavenly bliss. Those Gentiles who in the past accepted the Noahide law because of Jewish political rule qualified for the category of "resident alien" (*ger toshab*), meriting the right of domicile in the land of Israel and the general right of the protection of law. For what category do Gentiles qualify if they accept the Noahide law out of conclusions of practical wisdom?

At this point the respective manuscripts of *Hilkhot Melakhim* present two different readings. Some manuscripts, followed by the subsequent printed editions of the text, read as follows:

> But if he did them because of rational conclusion, he is not [*ayn zeh*] a resident alien or [*veayno*] one of the saints of the nations of the world, and is not one of their sages [*velo mehakhmehem*].[51]

Other manuscripts present the text of the last clause as stating, "but [*ela*] he is one of their sages."[52] With the manuscript evidence so divided, a conclusive reading cannot be drawn from it alone. Therefore, it seems to me that our method will have to be an examination of the structure of the passage both within its immediate context and, also, within the wider context of Maimonides' other remarks on the philosophy of law.

In terms of the immediate context of the passage, the positive inclusion of those who accept Noahide law on the basis of nonmetaphysical, or "utilitarian," reasoning in the category of Gentile "sages" (*hakhamim*) can be defended on the basis of symmetry. Maimonides designates three methods of accepting Noahide law: (1) political subservience, (2) religious submission, and (3) rational conclusion. The first method places one in the category of the resident alien. The second method places one in the category of the "saint." The way Maimonides sets up this correspondence between acts of acceptance and their respective categories indicates that there is a category corresponding to the acceptance of Noahide law because of rational conclusion. The second manuscript reading we noted thus completes the symmetry of this passage by placing this person in the category of Gentile *hakhamim*.[53] This is corroborated by the fact that several passages in the *Mishneh Torah* clearly indicate that Maimonides used the term *hakhamim* to designate persons possessing practical wisdom, be they Jews or Gentiles.[54] In the case of the Gentile who accepts Noahide law because of practical wisdom, we find a *hakham* who is morally adequate but metaphysically inadequate. Therefore, it seems to me, based on the contextual evidence and hermeneutical analysis, that Maimonides designated the person who accepts Noahide law based on practical wisdom to be a *hakham*. Maimonides recognizes as valid such a status but does not endorse it as exemplary.

Divine Law and Natural Law

During his analysis of the origins of law in general, which we have already examined, Maimonides concludes,

> Therefore I say that the Law, although it is not natural [*tib'it*], enters into what is natural [*mabo b'inyan hatib'i*]. It is part of the wisdom of the Deity with regard to the permanence [*beha'amid*] of this species of which He willed the existence, that He put into its nature that individuals belonging to it should have the faculty of ruling.[55]

In order to understand this important passage we must first understand what Maimonides means by "nature" (*teba'*).

In the *Guide* Maimonides uses the term *nature* in two different senses. On the one hand, he emphasizes that nature is the intelligent guiding principle within the created order.

> This is the meaning of nature ['*inyan hateba'*], which is said to be wise, having governance [*manhig*], caring for the bringing into existence of animals by means of an art of a craftsman [*bimlekhet mahshebet*], and also caring [*mashgiah*] for their preservation and permanence. . . . what is intended hereby is the divine thing [*ha'inyan haElohi*].[56]

Elsewhere he draws an analogy between nature as the conscious ordering function in the universe and nature as this same function in the human person.[57] On the other hand, he uses the term *nature* to designate necessity within the created order, that is, material which requires intelligent ordering.

> For the law always tends to assimilate itself to nature [*titdamah beteba'*], perfecting [*v'tashlim*] the natural matters in a certain respect [*al tzad ehad*]. For nature is not endowed with thought and understanding [*ba'al mahshabah vehistaklut*], whereas the Law is the determining ruling of the Deity [*vehanhagat Ha Shem*], who grants the intellect to all its possessors.[58]

Here we have a clear contradiction, so much so that most of the same terms are used in these two respective passages with directly contrasting meanings.

Maimonides uses the term *nature* ambiguously when describing man's condition because that condition is itself fundamentally ambiguous. On the one hand, man, like the heavens, is a rational being, capable of intellection. Man is the intelligible realm in miniature, the microcosm ('*olam katan*).[59] On the other hand, man, like the animals, is a sentient being having physical desires.[60] Now the term *nature* describes the state whereby any created being has reached the fullest perfection possible for it. Thus the term is used to describe the self-sufficient behavior of individual animals. Nature at this level is unconscious, that is, instinctual.

> None of the individual animals requires for its continued existence reflection, perspicacity, and the governance of conduct [*hanhagah*]. For it goes about and runs in accordance with its nature [*lefi tib'o*]. . . . Consequently the individual remains in existence during the time in which it exists, and the existence of the species [*mino*] continues.[61]

Maimonides goes on to indicate that were men to live on this individual instinctual level, they would quickly perish. Men require governance of their conduct (*hanhagah*). As we have seen, this governance is developed by intelligent political unity and order, law being the structure of the process. In other words, whereas sentient nature is sufficient for animals, it is insufficient for man because of his *political nature.* Man's political nature is his conscious striving for unity and order. This begins in his awareness of the especial precariousness of physical isolation among humans. As man's awareness develops, however, he is led to see how practical order in the political realm intends the rational order of the purely intelligible realm. Man's political nature, then, is the point at which human ambiguity is called into sharpest focus: physically man is an isolated animal; rationally he is a "species being" that participates in a fully unified intelligible realm.

Therefore, I think the contradiction in Maimonides' use of the term *nature* can be resolved if we specify what nature he means in any particular context. When he speaks of nature as an ideal for man, he means rational nature, that principle of governance which functions in either man, the *microcosm,* or the universe, the *macrocosm.* When, conversely, he speaks of nature as something requiring human improvement or development, then he means animal nature. In animals, nature requires no improvement, but since man is ambiguous or, to coin a term, "bi-natural," *his* animal nature must be *morally subordinated* to his rational nature. This moral subordination must not, however, obliterate the natural function of anything physical in human existence.[62] It must only limit the capacity of any physical drive to turn man's attention from reason to sensuousness.

This affects man's free choice. As we have already seen, man's freedom of choice is indicated by the uncertainty of his condition in the world. It is something he aspires to overcome. However, now that we understand the dual meaning of nature in Maimonides' system, what we might call "nature above" and "nature below," we can see why he contrasts freedom with nature. Freedom lies between these two natures. It attempts, when morally guided, to improve nature below by aspiring to nature above.[63]

This is why Maimonides contrasts things "natural" (*tibe'iyim*) with things "divine" (*Elohiyim*).[64] Moral law is what correlates these two realms, for it causes man, who begins in the lower realm, to aspire to the intelligibility of the higher realm. Furthermore, the complete morality of the prophet unifies this correlation by bringing the intelligibility of the higher realm down to the lower realm. Thus Maimonides' contrast between the divine realm and the political realm corresponds to his contrast between the natural, or physical, realm and the divine realm.[65] With this understood, we can understand Maimonides' characterization of the Torah as "entering into what is natural." This means that the Torah, as the correlation of the divine and human realms, has relevance for man's physical nature but cannot be reduced to it.[66] For if it were reduced to it, it could not very well guide it morally.

The Torah, then, transcends physical nature both in terms of its source and in terms of its end.[67] The Torah itself is intelligible even if it is not fully understood by the human intellect; physical nature is itself unintelligible. Therefore, the Torah is closer to the divine wisdom which willed the creation of the universe. The Torah also prescribes the ends of human striving: first, man's physical end, which is a stable, unified society; second, man's intellectual end, which is true knowledge of God.[68] In terms of the first end the Torah can be considered natural; in terms of the second it is divine.[69] Thus Maimonides refers to the physical end of the Torah as being "prior in nature and time."[70]

Noahide Law and Natural Law

The Torah is most evidently rational when its political function is most evidently manifest. It is least natural when its political function is least evidently manifest and, also, when the reasons for its particular details are most obscure. Understanding Maimonides' concept of nature enables us to designate the concept of Noahide law as a "natural law" theory, for the political function of Noahide law is more evidently manifest than any other group of laws presented in Scripture or tradition.

Let us see this natural law theory at work in Maimonides' explanation of two of the Noahide laws.

For Maimonides, the first Noahide law is the prohibition of idolatry ('abodah zarah). Maimonides considers the affirmation of the existence of God and the negation of idolatry to be the two intelligible foundations of the whole Torah.

> For these two principles, I mean the existence of the Deity and His being one, are knowable by human speculation alone [b'iyyun haenoshi], . . . by demonstration [b'mofet]. . . . As for the other commandments, they belong to the class of generally accepted opinions [mefursamot] and those adopted in virtue of tradition [v'hamekubbalot], not to the class of the intellecta [muskalot].[71]

Maimonides bases this on the talmudic view that the first two commandments of the Decalogue, namely, "I am the Lord your God" and "There shall be no other gods," were heard by all the people at Mount Sinai.[72] The rest of the commandments were transmitted through Moses. Maimonides interprets this distinction in the promulgation of the commandments to be due to a distinction among the commandments themselves. Also, for Maimonides the prohibition of polytheism and the affirmation of God's oneness are two sides of the same coin. Since God's oneness is known only negatively, as is the case with all the essential attributes of God, the prohibition of polytheism is an adequate expression of God's oneness. Maimonides equates idolatry with polytheism.[73]

In making this distinction between "intellecta" (muskalot) and "conventions" (mefursamot), Maimonides does not mean that only the affirmation of the existence and the oneness of God is intelligible and that all the rest of the commandments are, therefore, unintelligible.[74] Such an interpretation is clearly belied by Maimonides' continual treatment of the "reasons of the commandments" (ta'amay hamitzvot), wherein he went further than any of his rabbinic predecessors.[75] What Maimonides does mean, I think, is that only these two commandments are immediately intelligible per se because they deal with the essence of God, which is the unchanging foundation of all intelligibility.[76] The intelligibility of these two commandments, then, requires no external point of reference. They are ends in themselves and need not be justified by any external purpose.[77] The other commandments, conversely, all have a political context. They refer to various human actions. Their intelligibility is not immediate, because politics, with which they deal, is not an end in itself. Thus they are conceived of as *means* to other ends. The commandments have to be viewed either as serving a political purpose or as serving to eradicate idolatry. The other commandments, then, either serve to improve the body or to improve the soul. As such, they need to be both conventional and traditional precisely because Maimonides regarded society as a *sine qua non* for prophetic knowledge of God, the proper end of man. Society has both a horizontal and a vertical dimension. The horizontal dimension is ordered by present convictions; the vertical dimension is ordered by past traditions. We have seen that Maimonides viewed prophecy as the full human correlation of the divine and the political realms. The Torah, the product of Mosaic prophecy, thus correlates the intellecta and the conventions and traditions in one normative structure. At some times that correlation is more evident; at other times it is less so. It is most evident for the Noahide laws precisely because those laws are most general, containing few, if any, obscure details.

The second law which best illustrates Maimonides' natural law theory concerns forbidden sexual relations (*giluy 'arayot*).[78] Maimonides deals with this subject in terms of its political significance. In the *Mishneh Torah* he writes the following at the very beginning of his discussion of the laws dealing with sexual relations:

> Before the giving of the Torah a man would run into [*poge'a*] a woman in the marketplace. If they both desired that he take her [*liysa otah*], he would bring her into his house and copulate with her. . . . She is what is called a harlot [*kedeshah*].[79]

Maimonides' point is that before the Law was promulgated, sexual relations were informal and virtually unlimited. Also, they were not a matter of public control. The Law meant to limit their scope and their frequency. In the *Guide* Maimonides develops this position more explicitly and repeats the point he made earlier about the informality of sexual relations before the promulgation of the Law.

> Accordingly a single tribe that is united through a common ancestor . . . love one another, help one another, and have pity on one another; and the attainment of these things is the greatest purpose [*mikkavanot ha-Torah hagedolot*] of the Law. Hence harlots [*hakedesha*] are prohibited, because through them lines of ancestry are destroyed. . . . Another important consideration . . . is the prevention of an intense lust for sexual intercourse [*meni'at rob taavat hamishgal*] and constant preoccupation with it. . . . if harlots are permitted, a number of men might happen to betake themselves at one and the same time to one woman; they would inevitably quarrel; and in most cases they would kill one another or kill the woman.[80]

Thus Maimonides sees the normative limitation of sexuality as based on three reasons. (1) It strengthens the bond of kinship, which is the foundation of social cohesiveness and continuity. (2) It militates against violence, a chief cause of which is sexual jealousy. (3) It contributes to human rationality by containing excessive lust. All of this is structured by the public institution of marriage. Hence adultery is socially unacceptable because it destroys the bond of marital fidelity.

In the same chapter in the *Guide* Maimonides eliminates bestiality and homosexuality from the area of permitted sexual relations, because if even sexuality which is physically natural (*ha' inyan ha' tibe' i*) is permitted only for reasons of physical necessity (*letzorekh*), and even so is limited, then unnatural sexuality should be prohibited altogether because it serves no purpose. What Maimonides means, I think, is that heterosexuality is the physical basis of the family, which is the foundation of social cohesiveness and continuity. Homosexuality and bestiality serve no such purpose. Therefore they are only for the sake of pleasure (*ulebakesh hahanaah lebad*), which is thus experienced as an end in itself. For Maimonides they are unjustifiable precisely because they do not contribute to a higher end. Marital heterosexuality, on the other hand, is justifiable both because it makes a positive and necessary contribution to society and because it makes room for intellectual pursuits.

This double rationale, namely, that a law contributes both to physical and political well-being (*tikkun haguf*)[81] and to intellectual well-being (*tikkun hanefesh*) is not a double-effect theory. Rather, political well-being leads to intellectual well-being, and, on the other hand, an anti-intellectual, sensuous life leads to antipolitical activity. Although Maimonides follows Aristotle in distinguishing between moral excellence and intellectual excellence, and in making the former the stepping-stone to the latter,[82] he is much closer to Plato in his close correlation of these two ends. The following passage from the *Guide*, concentrating on the evils of excessive sensuousness, demonstrates this point:

> The lusts and licentiousness of the multitude . . . [are] what destroys man's last perfection [*shlemut haadam haaharon*], what harms him also in his first perfection [*shlemut harishon*], and what corrupts most of the circumstances of the citizens and of the people engaged in domestic governance. For only the desires are done, as is done by the ignorant; the longing for speculation [*hateshukot ha' iyyunot*] is abolished, the body is corrupted. . . . thus cares and sorrows multiply; mutual envy, hatred, and strife aiming at taking away what the other has, multiply. All this is brought about by the fact that the ignoramus regards pleasure alone as the end to be sought for its own sake [*takhlit mekhuvvenet l' atzmah*].[83]

As Maimonides had emphasized earlier in this section of the *Guide*, man's "first perfection" is intellectual. What he has shown here is that just as one cannot hope to achieve the "last perfection" without having achieved the first perfection, so without striving for the final intellectual happiness one cannot achieve even the earlier political happiness. The Torah, the product of Mosaic prophecy, comes to fully synthesize these two strivings.[84]

Hence we see that for Maimonides the rationale for the Noahide laws is either in terms of man's lower physical nature or in terms of man's higher intellectual nature. Noahide law, as the whole Torah *in potentia*, is natural law in its most immediately evident manifestation. Its generality and its lack of obscure details enable us to see the full correlation of divine wisdom and divine will. It is both knowable in itself (*ratio per se*) and known by all rationally moral persons (*ratio quod nos*).

Conclusion

The above analysis has, I think, shown us that Maimonides advocates an essentially rational, nondogmatic theory of law. It would seem that for Maimonides universal moral law does not require the affirmation of a particular historical revelation. All of this can be inferred from Maimonides' concept of prophecy, especially as stated in the *Guide*. Moreover, in a responsum to Rabbi Hasdai HaLevi the Spaniard, a responsum composed after the publication of both the *Mishneh Torah* and the *Guide*, Maimonides presents a clearly nondogmatic view of the possibility of Gentile apprehension, independent of historical revelation.

> You should know that "God desires the heart" [*Rahamana liba ba'ay*]. . . . thus the nations of the world have a portion in the world to come if they apprehend [*hesiygu*] what is capable of being apprehended in terms of knowledge of the Creator, blessed be He, and order their souls [*vehitkinu nafsham*] with good morals [*bamiddot hatobot*]. There is no doubt that whoever orders his soul with correct morals [*bekashrut hamiddot*] and correct wisdom about the faith of the Creator, blessed be He, surely such a person is one of the members of the world to come. . . . Indeed, the philosophers . . . call him a "godly man" [*ish Elohi*].[85]

In other words, the proper correlation of moral virtue and theological excellence can enable one to observe the *equivalent* of Noahide law *and* achieve eternal bliss. This possibility is acknowledged even by the philosophers, who reason independently without historical revelation. Being part of a historical community which acknowledges the authority of a historical revelation, preserving it and interpreting it, makes the achievement of eternal bliss easier by providing a traditional body of law and theology consistent with the true knowledge of God.[86] That is why Maimonides assigns to the Jewish authorities the task of enforcing Noahide law among the Gentiles whenever they have the political opportunity to do so.[87] However, what emerges from Maimonides' more philosophic treatment of the whole question of universal law is that being part of such a historical community, however morally and intellectually advantageous this may be, is not a *sine qua non* for the achievement of eternal bliss.

We thus see that Maimonides' theory of law, especially Noahide law, constitutes it as rational, revealed, and universal. The scope and the coherence of this theory attest to Maimonides' standing as a thinker of extraordinary Jewish learning and even more extraordinary philosophic insight.

NOTES

1. *The Jew and the Universe* (New York, 1936), p. 174.
2. Ibid., pp. 172–73.

3. See *Moreh Nebukhim* (hereafter MN), introduction; and Aristotle, *Metaphysics*, 983a1–10.

4. *Mishneh Torah* (hereafter MT), *Melakhim*, 9. 1.

5. In *Sefer Hamitzvot*, shoresh 2, Maimonides stipulates that commandments not *specifically* stated in the written Torah are not included among the 613. In MT, *Melakhim*, 9. 1, Maimonides carefully notes that the Noahide laws are *generally* indicated in Scripture.

6. For Maimonides' acknowledgment of his debt to Aristotle, see A. Marx, "Texts by and about Maimonides," *Jewish Quarterly Review* 25, no. 4 (April 1935): 379–80; and D. Novak, *Law and Theology in Judaism* (New York, 1974–76), 1:119; 2:190, n. 14.

7. MT, *Melakhim*, 9. 1.

8. For other examples of Maimonides' use of the term *hada'at noteh* to denote moral reasoning, see MT, *Yesoday HaTorah*, 5. 7; and *Gezelah Va'abedah*, 4. 16.

9. MT, *Melakhim*, 8. 11.

10. Maimonides notes, basing himself on the text from *Melakhim*, 8. 11, that a Gentile is rewarded by God only *if* he accepts a commandment because of his belief in Mosaic prophecy. See *Teshubot Harambam*, ed. J. Blau (Jerusalem, 1957), vol. 1, no. 148, pp. 282–84. Cf. *Melakhim*, 10. 10 and Radbaz thereto, quoting B. Kiddushin 31a; also MT, *Talmud Torah*, 1. 3; and commentary to M. Terumot 3. 9 and M. Makkot, end. None of this, however, implies that an act in compliance with Noahide law (or Torah law) but not performed from these theological motives is legally invalid. See B. Wein, *Hikray Halakhah* (Jerusalem, 1976), pp. 14–15, n. 12; 16–17; and D. Hartman, *Maimonides: Torah and Philosophic Quest* (Philadelphia, 1976), p. 260, n. 38.

11. See B. Pesahim 114b. For the debate on this general question, see Novak, *Law and Theology in Judaism*, 1:136 ff., 174, n. 10. On the other hand, Rabbi Jacob Emden (died 1776) concluded, in a response to a query from Moses Mendelssohn, that Maimonides held that the mitzvot qua commandments require kavvanah. Therefore, only Gentiles who observe Noahide law as revealed merit eternal bliss. See Moses Mendelssohn, *Schriften*, Jubilee ed. (Berlin, 1929–32), 16:180. However, this only implies that kavvanah affects the otherworldly consequences of the mitzvot. It does not imply that without kavvanah the acts themselves are valueless. See S. S. Schwarzschild, "Moral Radicalism and 'Middlingness' in the Ethics of Maimonides," *Studies in Medieval Culture* 11 (1977): 87, n. 64.

12. See MT, *Teshubah*, 3. 5. Maimonides' rabbinic sources seem to be T. Sanhedrin 13. 2 and B. Sanhedrin 105a. Furthermore, Maimonides himself cites *Mishnat Rabbi Eliezer*, ed. H. G. Enelow (New York, 1934), p. 121, as the source of his ruling. See *Teshubot Harambam*, ed. A. Freimann (Jerusalem, 1934), no. 124, p. 117. See also *Shemonah Perakim*, chap. 6, beginning; and MN 3. 51. For Maimonides' use of the term *hasidayhem*, see MT, *'Edut*, 11. 10.

13. *Hekhre'a Hada'at* is a rabbinic term denoting an inductive argument. See, e.g., P. Sanhedrin 1. 1; T. Hullin 8. 1. It should be contrasted with *Hekhre'a Hakatub*, that is, an argument based on Scripture. See, e.g., Sifra, ed. I. H. Weiss (Vienna, 1862), p. 1a. The difference between these two types of proof is based on the rabbinic distinction between *k'ra* and *sebara*. See, e.g., B. Berakhot 4b; B. Kiddushin 13b; and B. Abodah Zarah 34b. Also M. Guttmann, "Maimonide sur l'universalité de la morale religieuse," *Revue d'Études Juives* 99 (1935): 41. Maimonides' understanding of *hekhre'a hada'at* can be equated with his understanding of what in Arabic is called *kiyas*, that is, inductive-type estimation. See MN 2. 23 (beginning).

14. B. Pesahim 50b and parallels. See Maimonides, *Hakdamah L'Perek Helek*, ed. M. Rabinowitz (Jerusalem, 1961), pp. 114–17.

15. See MN, introduction.

16. MN 3. 45.

17. MN 2. 36, trans. S. Pines (Chicago, 1963), p. 369. (All Hebrew quotes are from Ibn Tibbon translation.)

18. See MN 1. 2.

19. MN 2. 36.

20. MN 1. 51, p. 112.

21. See Aristotle, *Physics*, 19416 ff.; and MN 2. 1.

22. See MT, *Teshubah*, 5. 5, for the assertion that free choice is prior to religious doctrine.

23. Ibid., 5. 4. See *Shemonah Perakim*, chap. 8.

24. See MN 3. 32.

25. See MN 2. 29.

26. Thus Maimonides in MN 1. 1 emphasizes intellect (*hasekhel ha Elohi*), not will, as the point in common between God and man. See MT, *Yesoday HaTorah*, 4. 8. This idea has many Jewish and non-Jewish expressions. See, e.g., Plato, *Phaedrus*, 248A; *Theaetetus*, 176A–B; *Laws*, 899D; Philo, *De Op.*, 69 (beginning); Epictetus, *Discourses*, 1. 9; and Clement of Alexandria, *Exhortation to the Greeks*, 10.

27. MN 3. 17, p. 469.

28. Note: "Choice [*proairesis*] is manifestly a voluntary act [*hekousion*]. But the two terms are not synonymous, the latter being the wider. Children and the lower animals as well as men are capable of voluntary action, but not of choice." Aristotle, *Nicomachean Ethics*, 1111b5, trans. H. Rackham (Cambridge, Mass., 1926), pp. 128–29.

29. *Shemonah Perakim*, chap. 1 (end).

30. See MN 1. 2.

31. MN 1. 69.

32. MN 2, introduction, no. 18; Aristotle, *De Anima*, 430a15, 431a1–5; and *Metaphysics*, 1049b25 ff. See A. J. Reines, *Maimonides and Abrabanel on Prophecy* (Cincinnati, 1970), pp. xxxi ff.

33. Maimonides' Neoplatonism came via Avicenna. For the difference between emanation and the four Aristotelian causes, see P. Morewidge, *The Metaphysics of Avicenna* (New York, 1973), pp. 264 ff. Cf. Thomas Aquinas, *Summa Theologiae*, 1, q. 79, aa. 3–4; q. 84, a. 4. Re the active intellect, see W. D. Ross, *Aristotle* (New York, 1959), pp. 146 ff.

34. MN 1. 65.

35. See *Sefer Hamitzvot*, neg. no. 365; and MN 2. 25, 3. 25–26, 31.

36. Thus, although Maimonides asserts that "there is a reason [*sibbah*]" for every commandment (MN 3. 26), there is more that we do not understand than we do understand (MN 3. 49). In terms of essence/function (*hokhmah*) we understand much; in terms of existence/entity (*ratzon*) we understand little. Maimonides is dealing with two types of teleology: functional teleology (which answers the question "How?") and existential teleology (which answers the question "Why?"). See Z. Diesendruck, "Die Teleologie bei Maimonides," *Hebrew Union College Annual* 4 (1928): 499 ff. Cf. Plato, *Republic*, 427B–C; and *Laws*, 738B–C.

37. Concerning the combination of wisdom and will in divine creativity as an artistic act a la Plato, *Philebus*, 26E–28D, see I. Efros, *Studies in Medieval Jewish Philosophy* (New York, 1974), pp. 164–65. For the suggestion that Maimonides' teleology, being more comprehensive than Aristotle's, has important affinities with the later thought of Plato (e.g., *Sophist*, 265C–E), see Diesendruck, *Die Teleologie bei Maimonides*; and his "Ha-Takhlit v'ha-Tearim b'Torat Harambam," *Tarbiz* 1, no. 3 (January 1930): 106 ff.

38. MN 1. 69, p. 170.

39. MN 2. 40, pp. 381–82.

40. For the influence of Avicenna on this point, see Pines's introduction to his translation of MN, p. xcix.

41. See commentary to M. Abodah Zarah 4. 6, where idolatry is portrayed as the mystical device used by political leaders to unify a community.

42. MN 2. 40, p. 384. See E. I. J. Rosenthal, "Torah and Nomos in Jewish Philosophy," in *Studies in Rationalism, Judaism, and Universalism: In Memory of Leon Roth*, ed. R. Loewe (London, 1966), pp. 218 ff.

43. See MT, *De'ot*, 3. 3, quoting M. Abot 2. 2; MN 1. 34; 2. 32, 36; 3. 8, 51.

44. MN 3. 34, p. 534. Both Plato (*Statesman*, 294A–C) and Aristotle (*Politics*, 1286a7 ff.) also recognize the generality of law. However, whereas for Maimonides this generality is the strength of law, bringing political unity out of individual diversity, for Plato and Aristotle it suggests that *who* the political leader is is more important than *what* the laws are, because a competent leader is better able than the laws to deal with individual cases and their respective peculiarities. See *Nicomachean Ethics*, 1132a20. For the importance of generality in talmudic jurisprudence, which undoubtedly influenced Maimonides' philosophy of law, see, e.g., M. Berakhot 1. 3 and Sifre, Debarim, ed. L. Finkelstein (Berlin, 1939), no. 34, p. 62, commenting on Deut. 6:7; B. Erubin 63b; B. Betzah 12a; B. Kiddushin 80a; B. Baba Metzia 39b; and Hullin 9a, 11a. Cf. Philo, *De Spec. Leg.*, 1. 3.

45. Concerning the immutability of the Torah, see MN 3. 41.

46. See MN 3. 18, 51.

47. The term *species being* is a deliberate use of Karl Marx's term *Gattungswesen* (see "Zur Judenfrage," *Werke* [Berlin, 1964], 1:370). I have chosen it because Marxist collectivism is probably more familiar to modern students than that of Maimonides. Both Maimonides and Marx regarded individualism as contrary to true human fullfillment. Of course, Maimonides and Marx were in essential disagreement as to what sort of society would be humanly fulfilling. For both, however, such a society was not yet a reality in history.

48. For the synthesis of intellection and imagination in the prophet, see MN 2. 37.

49. See MN 3. 54.

50. MN 2. 40, p. 382.

51. MT, *Melakhim*, 8. 11.

52. See S. S. Schwarzschild, "Do Noachites Have to Believe in Revelation?" *Jewish Quarterly Review* 52, no. 4 (April 1962): 302.

53. The form *'ayn . . . ela*, moreover, is extremely common in Tannaitic texts. See, e.g., B. Berakhot 5a commenting on Job 5:7.

54. MT, *Yesoday HaTorah*, 7. 1; and *De'ot*, 1. 4. Cf. *Teshubah*, 10. 2.

55. MN 2. 40, p. 382.

56. MN 2. 10, p. 272. See Pines's note 11 thereto.

57. MN 1. 72.

58. MN 3. 43, p. 571. Thus the commentator Rabbi Mosheh Narboni (circa 1350) explains Maimonides' remark, "The Law, although it is not natural, enters into what is natural" (MN 2. 40), as referring to the fact that "the languages are not natural." In other words, language as intelligent expression is not a manifestation of physical nature per se. Cf. Aristotle, *Politics*, 1253a10.

59. MN 1. 72. See Rabbi Joseph ibn Tzaddik (died 1149), *'Olam Katan*, an influential philosophic work devoted almost exclusively to this theme.

60. See MN 2. 23.

61. MN 1. 72, p. 190.

62. Thus Maimonides states that any pagan practice "required by speculation concerning nature [*ha'iyyun hatib'i*] is permitted" (MN 3. 37, p. 543). In other words, the law of the Torah does not contradict nature, as does idolatry, which prescribes "things not required by reasoning concerning nature [*heykesh hatib'i*]." See commentary to M. Pesahim 4, end; and MT, *Shabbat*, 19. 13, based on B. Shabbat 67a. Cf. MN 3. 20, 46.

63. This double use of the term *nature* has philosophic precedent in Aristotle, *Metaphysics*, 1015a15. See also Plato, *Republic*, 423D and 429A.

64. See MN 1. 34, 3. 51.

65. For Maimonides' insistence on the congruity of the Torah and reason precisely because both follow a "natural order," see *Maamar Tehiyyat Hametim*, chap. 6. Cf. Philo, *De Vita Mosis*, 2. 48.

66. See Novak, *Law and Theology in Judaism*, 1:144.

67. Thus it is incorrect to assume that Maimonides means here that the *end* of the Torah is natural (i.e., social), but its *source* is divine, as does Prof. José Faur in "Mekor Hiyyuban shel HaMitzvot L'Da'at HaRambam," *Tarbiz* 38 (1968): 51. The end of the Torah is determined by man's rational nature, not his social nature. Only the initial intelligibility of the Torah is social.

68. MN 3. 27. Maimonides sees the political end of the Torah exemplified in the virtue of "awe of God" (*yirat Ha-Shem*). See MN 3. 24, 52 (end). Just as the political end chronologically precedes the intellectual end, so does *yirat Ha-Shem* chronologically precede "love of God" (*ahabat Ha-Shem*). See MT, *Teshubah*, 10. 1–2; and MN 3. 24, 52 (end).

69. Whereas Professor Faur reads the text in MN 2. 40 too literally, Prof. Alvin J. Reines does not read it literally enough. He writes: "The Law is not natural in that it is the artificial creation of men; it enters into the natural by realizing the natural providential purpose" ("Maimonides' Concept of Mosaic Prophecy," *Hebrew Union College Annual* 40–41 [1969–70]: 359, n. 127). Maimonides does not ascribe the Torah to human invention but to Moses' unambiguous *normative* prophecy (see MN 2. 35, 39). The Torah's "entering into what is natural" refers to the Torah's relevance for man's physical/social nature. Its end, by contrast, is referred to as "divine" (see MN 1. 34, 2. 40).

70. MN 3. 27. Prof. Shlomo Pines, in his lucid introduction to his translation of MN, makes the important point that the philosopher is far more politically involved for Plato than he is for Aristotle (pp. lxxxvi–lxxxvii). Along these lines one should compare *Republic* 516C ff. and *Nicomachean Ethics* 1177bl; see D. Novak, *Suicide and Morality* (New York, 1975), pp. 22 ff.

71. MN 2. 33, p. 364.

72. B. Makkot 24a.

73. *Sefer Hamitzvot*, neg. no. 1.

74. Indeed, in his earliest work, *Millot Hahigayon*, ed. L. Roth (Jerusalem, 1965), sec. 8, pp. 44–45, Maimonides classified the concepts of *mefursamot* and *mekubbalot* as things clearly evident, not requiring proof for their existence. In MN 1. 51 he did not include them in this category. It would seem that as Maimonides' thought developed, he realized that even the more universally prevalent *mefursamot* were only true in a relative sense. In his mature thought he seems to have followed Aristotle more closely in seeing intelligible nature as a truer foundation for morality than *consensus gentium*. See Aristotle, *Nicomachean Ethics*, 1134b20; and *Rhetoric*, 1373b5. It would seem that the great project of Maimonides' philosophy of law was to ground the *mefursamot* of the Torah in the realm of the *muskalot*, thus giving them greater intelligibility by participation.

75. See MN 3. 31.

76. MT, *Yesoday HaTorah*, beginning.

77. See MT, *Abodah Zarah*, 11. 16.

78. In the MT, *Genebah*, 7. 12, Maimonides refers to *'arayot* as being a matter between man and God. Earlier, in the *Shemonah Perakim*, chap. 6, he classifies *'arayot* among the "traditional" (*shim'iyot*) commandments. However, he may well be referring to certain prohibited incestuous relationships whose particular rationale is not evident, rather than the general concept of incest, whose rationale is evident.

79. MT, *Ishut*, 1. 1, 4.

80. MN 3. 49, pp. 601–2.

81. MN 3. 27.

82. See *Nicomachean Ethics,* 1103a15.

83. MN 3. 33, p. 532. See 3. 11.

84. This complete synthesis must be the result of the most direct possible prophetic apprehension. Any mediation would lessen its simple unity and force. This is why, it seems to me, Maimonides emphasized points about Mosaic prophecy in contrast to other types of prophecy (MT, *Yesoday HaTorah*, 7. 6; and MN 2. 45). One main point is that only Mosaic prophecy is immediately normative (MN 2. 39). Here we see a logical connection between the descriptive and prescriptive aspects of Mosaic prophecy which corresponds to the intellectual and political aims of the Torah of Moses. Prophecy which is mediated, on the other hand, can only result in more tentative prescriptions. Thus the Mosaic law is not rooted in imagination (contra Reines, ''Maimonides' Concept of Mosaic Prophecy,'' pp. 353 ff.).

85. *Kobetz Teshubot HaRambam*, ed. A. Lichtenberg (Leipzig, 1859), 2: 23b–24a. See *Hakdamah L'Perek Helek*, ed. M. Rabinowitz (Jerusalem, 1961), p. 124 (top). As a Halakhist, however, Maimonides had to codify traditional sources that were quite dogmatic. See MT, *Issuray Biah*, 14. 4, based on B. Yebamot 47a.

86. See MN 3. 54.

87. MT, *Melakhim*, 8. 10.

Moses Mendelssohn's Political Philosophy

Alexander Altmann

Brandeis University

Moses Mendelssohn's role as a political philosopher has received scant attention hitherto. His fame has rested chiefly on his work as a metaphysician and as a pioneer in German aesthetics. True, his plea for toleration—a major theme in his *Jerusalem* (1783)—has been widely noted, yet it has hardly been seen as part of a more comprehensive political theory. Only in recent years has interest in Mendelssohn's political philosophy begun to stir. This paper seeks to contribute to an elucidation of this particular aspect of Mendelssohn's thought.

In concerning himself with political theory, Mendelssohn might seem to have followed a precedent set in medieval Jewish (and Islamic) philosophy in which politics was seen to be intimately related to the revealed law of religion and in which the Platonic figure of the lawgiver-king was considered to have found its consummation in Moses (or Muhammad). Within medieval Jewish philosophy the quest for the ideal or perfect state took the form of identifying the legislation of the Torah with this utopian ideal which had taken on the flesh of reality. Thus Maimonides diagnosed the Torah as the most "balanced"—hence most perfect—law, far superior to the man-made *nomoi* of the nations. Here the concern with politics was confined to the effort of investing the prophetically revealed Torah with the aura of indisputable authority. Politics was more or less an inner-Jewish matter of theological import, a means for securing the allegiance of Jews to the Torah. This view of politics fully corresponded to the situation and the needs of the Jewish people in the Diaspora. As an outsider vis-à-vis the host nations and bereft of all power to influence their decision-making processes in the realm of politics, the Jew would have been unrealistic had he busied himself with political thought in a more general sense. Yet it was precisely this wider concern that characterized Mendelssohn's preoccupation with politics, and he may therefore be described as having ushered in a new period in Jewish political thought, one no longer narrowly concerned with theologicopolitical necessities.

Mendelssohn's attitude was determined by an acute sense on his part that the time had come for Jews to make an effort to become politically integrated into the states in which they were domiciled—hence his overriding desire to evolve a political theory that would facilitate the emancipation of the Jews. The increasing secularization of the state had not yet resulted in any amelioration of the civil disabilities under which the Jews suffered everywhere. The idea of toleration had slowly emerged from the battles of the Reformation and had even penetrated into ecclesiastical law, where it bore the impress of seventeenth century Enlightenment notions. It had produced a grudging acknowledgment of the noncriminal character of heresy, and it had legally established the right of the major Christian denominations to coexist in peace. However, many categories of dissidents and, above all, the Jews (who were labeled "infidels") had not as yet been admitted to equal citizenship. It was in this area that Mendelssohn felt the urge to help in promoting human rights, and it was this "existential" concern that inspired much of his political writing. He did not wish to be regarded as a champion of his own people only, but made it clear that he was equally concerned with the rights of all the oppressed. He stressed the universalistic aspect of human rights not only as a human being but, primarily, as a philosopher whose domain comprised all of humanity.

What strikes one as a characteristic trait in all phases of Mendelssohn's life is the courage with which he expressed his political convictions. True, any possibility of political activism was ruled out by his precarious situation as a Jew bereft of civil rights and as a merely "tolerated" resident in Frederick the Great's Berlin. Reformist zeal was in any case a commodity in short supply at the time in Germany. Yet within the confines of this "quiet contentedness" with reality (as Hegel called it) Mendelssohn managed to go to the very limits of whatever liberal sentiment could be articulated. Thus, when invited by Isaac Iselin of Basel to join the Swiss Patriotic Society as a literary contributor, he movingly described the dual restrictions under which he labored as a monarchical subject and as a Jew. In a review article on Iselin's *Philosophical and Political Essays* he wrote in 1761 that only in a free state, that is, in a republic, could one articulate political thought in a frank and fearless manner. In a monarchy, Minerva (here symbolizing the Enlightenment) often had to "pull the helmet over her eyes so as to prevent her penetrating glance from seeing things not meant to be noticed." As a result of such pronouncements, Mendelssohn acquired the reputation of being a republican at heart. Count William of Schaumburg-Lippe, one of the most liberal minds of the eighteenth century, recorded in one of his recently published writings that "the great German philosopher Moses Mendelssohn" considered the "natural liberty of man" far better safeguarded in a republic or an aristocracy than in a monarchy. As late in his life as 1784 Mendelssohn made this rather revealing observation: "The question has been posed as to which form of constitution is the better, the monarchical or the republican. A much-lauded answer says: The monarchical, if the ruler is wise; the republican, if he is not. I, for my part, would say: The republican, if the people is wise; if it is not, the monarchical." Mendelssohn's preference for the republican form of government could not have been stated more clearly.

This undisguised option is but one aspect of the love of liberty which forms the essential element of Mendelssohn's political philosophy. The major concern of

Mendelssohn's political thought may be described as the desire to see as much of natural liberty preserved in the civil polity as was compatible with the purposes for whose sake that polity had come into being. Since, according to the prevalent political theory of the time, the civil polity had been founded by the social contract, Mendelssohn's endeavor may also be said to have been directed toward an interpretation of the social contract that would allow for the continued operation of natural law (which includes the affirmation of natural liberty, *libertas naturalis*) on the largest possible scale. The German natural law school that dominated the scene in Mendelssohn's day, to which he too subscribed, had been shaped by Samuel Pufendorf, Christian Thomasius, and, particularly, Christian Wolff, whose extensive *Jus naturae* Mendelssohn had studied assiduously in his younger days. That school had given due prominence to the concept of natural liberty, that is, to the liberty enjoyed by man in the precivil natural state (*status naturalis*), but it had given equal prominence to man's freely willed surrender of that liberty through the social contract. The security of life, limb, and property created by virtue of the social contract (*pactum sociale*) was paid for by the severe restriction of the freedom and independence inherent in the state of nature. While in England the Lockean interpretation of the social contract was meant to safeguard a maximum amount of natural freedom, the German natural theorists tended to condone a maximum amount of absolutism and to argue that for the sake of the public welfare (*salus publica*) individual people's liberty inevitably had to be sacrificed in large measure. In a monarchy, they argued, only the prince retained natural liberty to the full, and he was not answerable to his subjects for the way in which he looked after their welfare. He knew best what was in their best interests, and they had to be ready to obey him. It was only toward the end of the eighteenth century that a more liberal stance developed in Germany, as has recently been shown in an excellent study of the subject by D. Klippel. What has not been considered is the possibility that Mendelssohn's advocacy of more liberal principles may have had some influence on this development.

What, then, was Mendelssohn's view of the state's purpose and of the underlying motive for the social contract by which the state comes into being? Since, as we have mentioned, it is the natural law which Mendelssohn wants to survive as much as possible under the changed conditions of the polity, we have to look, in the first place, at his concept of natural law in the state of nature. One obvious and universally recognized element of natural law is the right of self-defense, which stems from the natural urge toward self-preservation and finds legal expression in the negative norm not to hurt anybody (*neminem laedere*). Natural law, operating as it does without the benefit of law courts and authorized sanctions, vindicates the individual's right to judge his own case and to execute punishment. Mendelssohn gave its full due to this principle, but he gave equal recognition to another, positive element of natural law, namely the obligation to actively benefit others, which had been defined as a ''duty of humanity'' (*officium humanitatis*) or a ''duty of

33

conscience'' rather than as a legal obligation. Mendelssohn adopted the current terminology by which duties of conscience had come to be differentiated from the more strictly legal obligation not to violate the rights of others. The latter he called a ''perfect'' duty, the former an ''imperfect'' one. Perfect duties are coercible and their neglect is punishable, whereas imperfect duties cannot be imposed by force and their infringement carries no penalty, remains a matter of conscience alone. A poor man may beg for alms. His right to do so is a perfect right. Yet the rich man's duty to support him is only an imperfect duty. The rich man's noncompliance with that duty is no breach of law and cannot be construed as punishable.

This set of categories had been spelled out first by Pufendorf and had been amply discussed by Wolff. What Mendelssohn added to it was an emphasis on two aspects of the duties of conscience. (1) Man's happiness is inseparable from their fulfillment. In Mendelssohn's phrase, ''man cannot be happy without active benevolence.'' Benevolence benefits both the beneficiary and the benefactor. In contrast to the gloomy picture which Hobbes drew of the nature of man, the ''war of all against all'' being the ''state of nature,'' Mendelssohn viewed benevolence as a fundamental disposition of natural man. He welcomed Rousseau's portrayal of man in the natural state as capable of pity, which, to him, was a manifestation of love. What he rejected in Rousseau was the latter's denial of reason and natural law as operative in the state of nature. In Mendelssohn's view there had never been an actual primordial state of nature, let alone a state of nature of either the Hobbesian or the Rousseauan variety. The term *state of nature* (status naturalis) did not designate a historical phase but signified a mental construct, a model by which one depicted the legal realm that had validity in the absence of any contractual agreements and authorized law courts; in other words, the state of nature was tantamount to the human condition prior to any civil order and ruled solely by natural law. This basic human condition Mendelssohn regarded as one in which happiness was possible as a result of benevolence. (2) Happiness as just defined depended on man's liberty to benefit whom and when and to what extent he desired. Since man's capacity for benefaction was not unlimited, his conscience had to decide upon the object and the manner of his good deeds. In the liberty to make decisions of this kind and to choose the right action in conflictual situations, Mendelssohn saw a ''major portion of man's happiness'' within the state of nature. Natural liberty meant for him, first and foremost, the freedom of man to act according to his own lights when faced with conflicting claims upon the goodness of his heart. Whereas most German jurists of the natural law school considered natural liberty to consist in independence, that is, in not being subject to another's sovereignty (*imperium*), Mendelssohn gave natural liberty a more positive connotation. It meant the unrestricted right to follow one's own conscience in the discharge of benevolence.

Why should man have abandoned the state of nature and put up with the restrictions on his liberty that resulted from entering into the social contract? This question, which lies at the root of modern political theory, assumes a special urgency in Mendelssohn's case. While the need for political order and state power is obvious for Hobbes, and even for Locke and Pufendorf, all of whom assume a state of nature beset by disorder and infirmity of varying degree, Mendelssohn's near-idyllic picture of the *status naturalis* does not seem to call for any such drastic change as is implied in the establishment of the polity. The answer given by him is, again, highly characteristic of his moral stance. In Mendelssohn's view it is the larger scope offered to the exercise of man's manifold gifts and talents, including his political propensities, that urges man to leave the lonesome state of nature or whatever primitive society he may have found himself in and to seek the more fulfilling life of a fully organized society (state and society being almost synonymous terms in the eighteenth century). According to Mendelssohn, as soon as man realizes that societal life holds out greater scope for his potential growth as a human being, that happiness is a matter of more diversified activity, that man is not meant to live in isolation, he will understand that the loss of natural liberty entailed by the social contract will be amply compensated for by the gain in human stature which life in an organized society promises. The social contract is therefore the "exodus" from narrow constriction to selfishness. It completes the process of winning access to larger perspectives that was begun by such simpler forms of contractual agreements as marriage, tribal union, and the village. The reason for Mendelssohn's eagerness to advance Jewish civil rights was no doubt his awareness of the need to present larger opportunities to the woefully stifled talents of his nation. How deeply he felt the denial of such opportunities is apparent from many of his private and public utterances.

Yet, while highlighting the valuable benefits of the social contract, Mendelssohn insisted that the unavoidable limitation of individual liberty in the state had to be kept within strictly controlled bounds. Thus, he counseled against a state-regimented welfare system that would do away with the private exercise of charity and benevolence. He insisted that the great boon provided by voluntary benefactions had to be safeguarded. Human happiness, he pointed out, depended on the measure of freedom granted to individual initiative in the realm of duties of conscience. Not all such "imperfect" obligations should be transformed into "perfect," that is, coercible, duties. Moreover, the citizens ought to understand that in complying with whatever compulsory obligations devolved upon them as members of the commonwealth they could still recapture a sense of freedom and personal decision once they realized that life in the polity meant more gain than loss, that the state provided not merely protection of life and property (as Hobbes, Locke, and Pufendorf had suggested) but a chance for a better, happier form of existence. What Mendelssohn meant to convey was the awareness that the social contract represented something more than the fiction of a one-time act creating the state, that it was an ever-renewed compact by which the obligations accepted became duties entered into again and again. It seems obvious that Mendelssohn, the ardent lover of liberty, sought to remove the sting of compulsion from the consciousness of the citizen.

In an endeavor to secure the survival of natural law amid the more complex reality of statehood, Mendelssohn also insisted that the state had no authority to enact legislation in conflict with the principles of natural law. All that the state could legitimately do was to pass laws which transformed imperfect rights and duties into perfect (coercible) ones. It could not create new categories of rights and duties. It was bound by the basic structure of natural law. This bold theory did not go unchallenged. Such an influential protagonist of natural law as the jurist Ludwig J. F. Höpfner opposed Mendelssohn's theory as too radical. Others, however (e.g., the young Friedrich Gentz, whom Mendelssohn had introduced to Kant and who later rose to fame as Count Metternich's political adviser), seem to have adopted the theory. It is quite clear what Mendelssohn intended by advancing such a far-reaching doctrine. He wanted to prevent any lapses into legislation that would annihilate fundamental human rights. His sentiments were not far from those that inspired the American Declaration of Independence, and they have been reechoed in our own age by such political thinkers as Leo Strauss and John Courtney Murray, while legal positivists such as Hans Kelsen have rejected the natural law concept altogether.

The notion of "human rights" (*Rechte* or *Gerechtsame der Menschheit*) was close to Mendelssohn's heart. It underlies his impassioned plea for the civil admission of the Jews and for the complete toleration of all dissidents in his preface to the German edition of Manasseh ben Israel's *Defense of the Jews* (1782) and in his *Jerusalem* (1783). The *Jerusalem* (which contains a most enlightening excursus on natural law) offers an entirely novel approach to the philosophic vindication of toleration and liberty of conscience. It rests on the assumption that the right to decide on what opinion to hold *was not* surrendered in the social contract because such a right *cannot* be forfeited. It is inalienable. This being the case, the state can have no control over opinions nor can it arrogate to itself the right to reward by certain privileges the holders of one set of opinions (religious beliefs) and to penalize by the imposition of civil disabilities the representatives of other opinions. Mendelssohn agreed with Locke, however, that atheists (whose oaths cannot be trusted) are unfit for toleration. Apart from this exception, he denied the legitimacy of any concern on the part of the state for the religious beliefs of its citizens. What alone matters from the commonwealth's point of view is the morality of its members, not the dogmatic creed in which moral principles may be enshrined. To be more precise: The state is interested in religion only insofar as the latter promotes the moral way of life, and it must be opposed to any attempt on the part of a religion to usurp the coercive prerogatives imparted to the state by virtue of the social contract. Hence Mendelssohn sternly opposed the exercise by either church or synagogue of disciplinary measures such as excommunication.

Mendelssohn's concept of religion seems to have been largely influenced by

Thomasius's complete spiritualization of the Christian religion as distinct from Judaism, in which religion and state were originally linked in an indissoluble unity and every offense against God's Law was punishable by state authority. In Protestant ecclesiastical law the kings of Israel were often portrayed as "custodians" of religion and as examples to be followed by the Christian kings. Against this trend Thomasius had stressed the difference between the ancient Jewish religion and the Christian religion, a difference that in his view militated against any comparison between the respective roles of the Israelite kings and the Christian kings. According to Thomasius, the Christian religion was utterly nonpolitical, noncoercive, and Christian princes had to be purely political in their concerns, without trying to rule the church or meddling in churchly matters. In his *Jerusalem* (subtitled *Religious Power and Judaism*) Mendelssohn tried to show that the original union of state and religion which characterized the Mosaic legislation eventually broke down and was tacitly abandoned as a result of the destruction of the second Jewish commonwealth. Judaism had therefore assumed the character of a purely spiritual faith. True, Mendelssohn, in part 2 of his *Jerusalem,* defined Judaism as a "revealed legislation" in addition to its system of beliefs, which contained nothing beyond the tenets of natural religion, that is, the affirmation of God's existence, providence, and final reward and punishment in the afterlife. As a "revealed legislation," Judaism might appear to bear the attributes of a legalistic (state-backed) entity rather than of a merely moralistic one. If this interpretation were correct, Mendelssohn would have led us back in part 2 to a concept of religion discarded in part 1, where the spiritual nature of "true religion" had been pointed out. Yet the contradiction is only on the surface. What Mendelssohn means by the "revealed legislation" of Judaism is a body of precepts enjoining ritual and symbolic acts by which the eternal verities of natural religion (which form the beliefs of Judaism) are constantly brought to our attention. There is nothing legalistic, let alone political or coercive, about those precepts. Judaism, as Mendelssohn conceives it, is ideally and historically as "spiritual" as Thomasius's version of Christianity—and far more rational. It therefore fits beautifully into the modern state, which is no longer a Christian but a secular state.

As is well known, Kant hailed Mendelssohn's *Jerusalem* as "the announcement of a great, though slowly advancing, reform which will affect not only the Jewish nation but others too." It has been demonstrated in recent research that Kant's famous essay on the nature of the Enlightenment was stimulated by the *Jerusalem,* and there are many other evidences of the impact that Mendelssohn's work had upon the political thinking of the period. There has also been cumulative testimony to the great respect in which Mendelssohn's political ideals were held by the members of the illustrious Berlin Wednesday Society, of which he was a member. Finally, it is becoming increasingly clear that Mendelssohn's influence on the form and substance of the "Prussian Common Law," the great legislative enterprise of the era of Frederick the Great, is not to be gainsaid. For all of these reasons it may not be too sanguine to declare that Moses Mendelssohn's place in the evolution of liberalism in the late eighteenth century in Germany seems to be assured.

NOTES

For sources, see the following publications of the author:

"The Quest for Liberty in Moses Mendelssohn's Political Philosophy," in *Lessing Yearbook,* vol. 12, part 2 (scheduled to appear in 1981).

"Toleranz und Gewissensfreiheit: Eine begriffsgeschichtliche Untersuchung," in *Mendelssohn-Studien,* ed. Cécile Lowenthal-Hensel and Rudolf Elvers (Berlin, 1979).

"Mendelssohn on Excommunication: The Ecclesiastical Law Background," in *Sefer Ya'akov Katz* (Jerusalem, 1980).

The *Book of the Covenant:*
An Eighteenth Century Quest
for the Holy Spirit

Monford Harris

Spertus College of Judaica

Phineas Elijah Hurwitz's *Book of the Covenant* (Sefer Habrith), first published anonymously in 1797 and expanded and republished in 1807, was one of the most widely read Jewish books in modern Jewish history. Both European and Mediterranean Jewry were attracted by this book. Its popularity did not wane until recent times. There are men alive today who can remember this book being read as entertaining and pious reading for Sabbath afternoons, just as there are those who can remember being told in their youth that it was not necessary to study at a *gymnasium* since all secular knowledge was contained in the *Book of the Covenant*. It contained something for everybody. As Hurwitz himself noted, some readers thought it had been written by Moses Mendelssohn, and others thought it had been written by the Gaon of Vilna. That such divergent authorship could be attributed to the *Book of the Covenant* is of great importance. The mistaken ascriptions of authorship tell us much about the readers it appealed to: it appealed to the enlightened Jew—hence the "authorship" of Mendelssohn; it appealed to the traditional Jew—hence the "authorship" of the Gaon of Vilna.

Modern Jewish scholarship also seems to be somewhat uncertain about Hurwitz. It seems to be uncertain whether a man permeated by the spirit of Mendelssohn or a man permeated by the spirit of the Gaon wrote the *Book of the Covenant*. This places modern scholarship somewhat in the situation of the readers of its first edition, who read it without knowing the author's name. All subsequent readers have known the author's name but have not been quite able to make up their minds as to what Phineas Elijah Hurwitz was about.

It will be our contention that although Hurwitz may have had within himself certain unresolved ambiguities, for he was a product of a transition period in Jewish history, he nevertheless knew clearly where he stood and what he hoped to accomplish by writing the *Book of the Covenant*. Hurwitz did not aspire to write an original work, for he saw himself as a "modern" commentator to sixteenth century mystical treatises—an issue to which we shall return. Yet what Hurwitz did was to write an original tour de force. This made the *Book of the Covenant* a success in that it attracted many, many readers, but at the same time it made the book a failure.

Its standing as an original tour de force, its great popularity, its ultimate failure—these are the qualities that make the *Book of the Covenant* interesting for the historian of ideas. In discussing the study of the history of ideas, Arthur O. Lovejoy says, "Your minor writer may be as important as . . . the authors of what are now regarded as the masterpieces. . . . 'The tendencies of an age appear more distinctly in its writers of inferior rank than in those of commanding genius. These latter tell of past and future as well as of the age in which they live. They are for all time. But on the sensitive responsive souls, of less creative power, current ideals record themselves with clearness.'" In this sense Phineas Elijah Hurwitz, a "minor writer," is of historic interest.

The *Book of the Covenant* is a long book containing nearly 400 closely printed pages. It is written in an unpretentious Hebrew which Hurwitz translated from Yiddish, Hurwitz's native language. It is divided into two parts: the first deals with the natural world, the world of science; the second deals with the supernatural world, the world of Kabbalah.

Hurwitz sees his book as embodying two kinds of wisdom, the wisdom of science and the wisdom of Kabbalah. He views it as a work in the tradition of the Solomonic sage, and for him this book of wisdom is a unified work.

The part of the book which deals with science is longer than the part which deals with Kabbalah. But the separation of the two subjects is not absolute. Religious statements and attitudes permeate the section on science.

Hurwitz tells us that all his facts and ideas "are copied from the books of the wise men among the nations; [such material] has as yet not been incorporated into Hebrew books except for some very minor exceptions here and there." However, he does not mention any specific scientific sources.

On this level, Hurwitz is an eclectic and a popularizer, not an original thinker. He, of course, accepts the idea of *creatio ex nihilo*. He accepts, and discusses at length, the concepts of form and matter as basic to the structure of the universe. He takes seriously, and uses, the ancient-medieval idea of the four elements: fire, air, water, earth. These four elements serve to structure the first part of his book. Under each of these headings he discusses various topics, ranging from the sky which overarches the earth to man, some of his diseases, some of his good practical inventions, and aspects of Jewish faith and history. We shall not outline in dreary detail this part of the book. Our concern is with Hurwitz's basic assumptions and his ultimate goal. But in order to better understand the temper of his work, it would be of value to cite some of the more interesting examples of what interested him in the realm of "science."

Scattered throughout one finds do-it-yourself hints on how to make simple scientific instruments: a thermometer, a prism, a water pump, a barometer. He is convinced of the value of the thermometer, for the person who has one will not waste money in overheating his house and will be able to prevent much sickness. Practical inventions and discoveries fascinate Hurwitz. He devotes two pages to lightning rods; he is interested in the microscope, sleeping bags, balloon flight, the parachute, and preventive medicine. The problem of smallpox is of particular concern to him, for he devotes three and a half pages to it. He mentions Jenner and discusses his vaccine. He urges all Jews to use it, for the contemporary rabbinic sages have authorized its use. He explains the process of vaccination.

The do-it-yourself advice which Hurwitz gives throughout the first part of his book presents something of a question. Did he actually make the instruments and conduct the experiments he mentions, or are the directions he gives simply quotations from books? Our guess is, and it can only remain a guess, that he had acted on at least some of his suggestions to his readers. First of all, he seems to be a man who always knows what he is about. There is a feeling of sureness about his book. He seems to have a grasp of things. Second, he has about him a youthful enthusiasm for this world. This is hard to demonstrate with any one quotation, but the first part of his book is permeated with a subtle excitement about a new world discovered. He may have discovered it through reading; but if so, reading was his portal to reality. And it became a fresh, wonderful world to him. Our impression, therefore, is that Hurwitz himself may very well have done some of the things he advised his readers to do.

The first four sections of the first part deal with astronomy. Hurwitz discusses, among other things, Herschel's discovery of Uranus, the question of whether there is human life on the heavenly bodies (he concludes that there is none), the poles, the sun encircling the earth (though he is aware of Copernicus and the alternative view), and the predictability of eclipses.

He then turns to the earth and the things that are involved with earth, air, fire, and water. This makes up the bulk of the first part of the book. And it includes a lengthy discussion on man. Of the things on earth he discusses are such matters as volcanoes, the sea, the continents, the Eskimo, Jewish exile, earthquakes, clouds, and rain. He provides some information of popular interest on such animals as apes and beavers—for example, how beavers build their houses. Finally, he takes up man, his physiology, his psychology, and the problems of knowledge, of faith, and of man's ultimate meaning. This concludes the first part of the book.

Having presented this briefest of summaries of the first 246 pages of the *Book of the Covenant,* we will now attend to the basic premises and assumptions, the structure of ideas rather than the bits of information, that are revealed in these pages. For these matters are part of an approach to the ultimate meaning of the book, which is the concern of our study.

Does Hurwitz side with the medieval thinkers or with the moderns? His attitude to Copernican astronomy is the first clue to the answer to this question.

> The earth stands firm in the center of all. This is the attitude of all the ancients, both of the Jewish and Gentile sages. . . . True, the investigator Copernicus . . . says the earth is not the center of all the spheres. The earth [etc.] moves around it, . . . which rests according to him like the midpoint in the circle. There was one already in ancient times who said this, Pythagoras. . . . His opinion was not then accepted by people. It was forgotten. Copernicus

had reestablished it and taught it. . . . He succeeded in this, for as of now practically all the Gentile sages have accepted it.

At this point Hurwitz gives a brief summary of the Copernican system.

But I shall not be as one who has not heard and as one who has no counterarguments. By the grace of God I have the power to demonstrate clearly that the view of Copernicus is false. I will tell all [Gentile and Jew]. . . . First I come with the strength of Tycho Brahe, who said to Copernicus, "If the earth rushes from east to west, it should follow that a stone falling from a high tower, from the west side, should not fall straight down but all quite a distance toward the west."

Hurwitz goes on to explain why this is so and records the give-and-take between Copernicus and Tycho Brahe, awarding the victory to the latter.

And even though it is true that [Brahe] does not succeed in the acceptance of his ideas in this era, who knows, perhaps his time will come in some future generation. . . . And then they will say, "There was once a man named Tycho Brahe . . . whose words were not accepted by his contemporaries because their instruments were not as good as those that we have. Of course in our time there has been much investigation, and through instruments which our ancestors knew nothing about, our wisdom has become greater than the wisdom of antiquity. And we know that he was right."

Hurwitz's generally optimistic view of the future of science is something we shall discuss.

This future knowledge will be right. . . . the rejoinder of Brahe to Copernicus was true for anyone who understands and loves truth. . . . This is my first answer, which is Tycho Brahe's answer, not my own.

Hurwitz addresses this "first answer" to Gentiles. By this he means that the answer is of universal import, for he could not have believed that his book would actually be read by Gentiles. He then goes on to present specifically Jewish answers to the Copernican view. Using a dialogic style, he starts by challenging the Jewish believer in Copernicanism to tell him why the Bible should use terms that are false (that is, non-Copernican). The Torah speaks the language of men, that is, resorts to anthropomorphisms, only when there is no other way to make its message comprehensible to men. But in this case the Torah could have spoken the truth, which would not have been too difficult for the people to understand. "From the mouths of Moses, Joshua, David, Solomon, and the prophets of the truth, would we not have accepted this [truth]? From the mouth of Copernicus [only] should we accept [it]?" He now begins a more aggressive attack against the Jewish proponent of Copernicanism:

Everybody, even a child, knows that the heavens and all they contain are not *our* world. The earth was given to man (Psalm 115). If the Copernican view is right, then the earth encircling the sun will have to enter the sun's sphere, which is the second heaven. Who can be foolish enough to believe that the earth, the lowly one among the exalted, can become so elevated. It is shameful for anyone to believe so.

Despite his rejection of Copernicus, however, Hurwitz sides with the moderns. In the first introduction he says this clearly: "At times, if you find some criticism of some ancient sage who is so superior to me, do not wonder as to how inferior persons can rise up against such sages. This is the way of a midget who, astride the shoulders of a giant, sees far-off things that the giant, despite his height, cannot see."

He expects new discoveries to result from better instruments. In commenting on Herschel's discovery of Uranus, he says, "Perhaps in the next generation more planets will be discovered since they will have better telescopes than we have today. In later times they will know about many planets." It should be noted that he adds that the talmudic sages knew all of these things through the holy spirit or through ancestral tradition but did not mention them because they were of no practical importance.

In any case, Hurwitz is optimistic about the future of science.

In discussing geography, he says, "There is no truth in what the early investigators, both Jewish and Gentile, say about the distribution of human habitation being restricted to eighty-two degrees; we know from travelers of the wide distribution of human population." He mentions Columbus's discovery of America and then discusses why that discovery was made in modern times.

> The reason that they found this in these latter generations is that there increased in the world profound wisdom concerning the secrets of nature, particularly wisdom concerning the sailing of boats, . . . their direction through the use of the compass, fixed by a magnet. Today's wisdom is ten times greater than the wisdom of all ancient men, who found it necessary to spend three years going to Ophir.

Since Hurwitz refers here to Hiram and Solomon's joint enterprises, the implication is that the moderns are superior to Solomon.

The wide distribution of human population, that the underside of the globe is inhabited, was not known, he says, either by the early philosophers or by many Jewish sages. He is somewhat embarrassed by this. Consequently he is forced to explain away the modern achievement.

> It is not that we have more knowledge than the ancients. Truly the understanding of the ancients is broader than ours. Verily, time has been the cause; for new lands have been discovered, with God's will, in the later generations. Wisdom has expanded through sustained study over a large span of time and through the discovery of marvelous instruments; as the saying goes, the wisest sage is time.

However, it is only when the early Jewish sages are mistaken that Hurwitz tempers his modernism; for his Jewish views are related to the rest of the work, as we shall see. He does not temper his modernism in deference to the mistakes of the ancient Gentile sages.

But Hurwitz, even with his great concern to protect the wisdom of the Jewish sages of the past, does remain among the moderns, for he is very critical of

Maimonides. And once Maimonides has been rejected, modern thought has a chance of coming into its own.

Hurwitz's optimism about modern science does not imply that he absolutized the findings of his times.

> Do not say that the earlier sages were not as wise as the later sages. For the earlier ones were like those that unlock the outer hall. They were far superior to us. But experience denies their words and opinions. The very same thing that happened to the early sages will happen to the sages of these generations. Another generation will blot out all they established. For their children will rise after them and will discover even more wonderful instruments and even better experiments, denying the [earlier] ideas, rejecting all their conclusions in matters based on philosophic knowledge built on the wings of theories of human reason. . . .
> All secular knowledge is far from the truth except for arithmetic and geometry. As for the rest, they are a will-o'-the-wisp.

Thus the science of any generation is not final. The knowledge of one generation is rejected by the next generation because the next generation has better instruments and techniques. In arguing that Copernicus was wrong and in stating why he believed that Tycho Brahe's contentions substantiated his own point of view, Hurwitz also gave expression to the optimism which led him to believe that later generations would validate Brahe's standpoint in some conclusive way. There he envisioned the finality of science. In the preceding quotation, however, he presents a view of the restless progression of science. That progression was made possible by casting off the shackles of the past, by a *Zeitgeist* which gave rise to new instruments and new experiments, such as seafaring.

Just as the absolutizing of the past by previous generations was wrong, so too the absolutizing of the present was wrong. Hurwitz therefore took to task a person whom he had quoted approvingly for casting off the shackles of the past.

> I saw that the philosopher Mendelssohn boasted in the introduction to his commentary to the *Guide for the Perplexed,* saying that philosophy had reached its fullness in his time. This is not surprising; in all the early generations the philosophers thought the very same, particularly at the time of Aristotle, yet the following generations always rejected their words and their opinions. On the contrary, in our very own time there has arisen a wondrous, famous sage, Kant, who destroyed the very foundations of the philosophers, broke down their fences, destroyed their very pillars and joints. He composed a remarkable book which served to deflate all their personal claims.

Therefore, the philosophy of the present time, like the philosophy of the past, had no right to make absolute claims.

As a moralist, Hurwitz considers himself to be a modern. He rejects an ethics based on fire-and-brimstone threats. There is implied a kind of naturalistic ethics that will appeal to the decent reader. This too is part of the modern temper in Hurwitz. Just as time will bring forth new scientific instruments which will make for new knowledge—the scientific optimism—so will the ethical impose itself on the reader, on the basis of naturalistic knowledge. There is no necessity for threats or authority.

Both these attitudes imply a break with the past.

It would not be correct, however, to judge Hurwitz as being fully among the moderns. The overwhelming tenor of his work is modern, but there are other aspects to the *Book of the Covenant*. For example, Hurwitz believes in demons. He refers to a "kind of demon called dragon" which is afraid of thunder and lightning, and so runs away and hides. The very source of this statement betrays his nonmodernism. For his source is *Sefer Hasidim*. So he trusts a book which he certainly knew was medieval to give him "scientific" information.

Basically, then, it would seem that while Phineas Elijah Hurwitz was among the moderns, his thought contained medieval elements. It might seem that the solution to this apparent contradiction is to say that he was, ideologically, a marginal man standing on the dividing line between the medieval and modern eras. Such a person, we would say, is bound to have contradictory views. But there is another possibility which we shall present after we have explored the *Book of the Covenant* more fully.

Man is an extremely important subject for the *Book of the Covenant*. It is more involved with man than with any other *natural* phenomenon. This involvement is not to be understood as deriving primarily from its modernism but from its Jewishness. The interest in man in Jewish thought, a complex issue, is far older than the eighteenth century. Isaiah Horowitz (1555–1630) was obviously not influenced by Alexander Pope's *Essay on Man* (written 1733–34) when at the beginning of his *Two Tablets of the Covenant* he wrote, "How awesome is man," and proposed to study this matter. "How awesome is man" is a quotation from midrashic sources. Lurianic Kabbalah, as we shall note, is also concerned with the problem of man.

Hurwitz's interest in man, then, did not derive primarily from modern sources, though he was undoubtedly influenced by them. His was a Jewish interest, particularly kabbalistic, with its own specific interests in man.

About one-third of the first part of the *Book of the Covenant* and, in a sense, all of the second part are concerned with man. In his discussion on man in the first part, Hurwitz mentions such things as inoculation for smallpox, anatomy, the senses, dreams, intuition, the problem of knowledge, faith and reason, and man's final goal.

Phineas Elijah Hurwitz was sensitive to the issue that is now called "mental health." The discussion of dreams, in which he raises the question of prophecy, quite logically brings him to the subject of mental aberrations.

> Among most of our people there is a very stupid custom. When something happens to a person as the result of a sickness in the brain or a distemper, then immediately he is called mad or dybbuk; they say [of him] that there is another spirit in him which comes from the evil one. Then they call a *baal shem tov* for him or a wizard to save him from his sickness. Were they wise, they could understand that they are harming him even more, that he will become even sicker. The truth of the matter is that it is like the dream; it comes through the imagination. . . . For after some sickness the very fine veins in the brain, called nerves,

> become closed as a result of some sickness in one of the humors; then rationality departs
> . . .; all that is left in the person is imagination itself. . . . And when he wishes to describe
> the bodily pain, he imagines that some destroyer—a man or some other creature [—is
> terrifying him]. . . . The demons do not know of such things.

Fear causes these imaginations. And to prove how powerful imagination can be, he states that the pregnant woman's imagination influences the child's appearance. So imagination is extremely powerful. The family of the sick man believes in the reality of all that he sees, the demon, or evil spirit, or Satan. "A fool believes anything: so they waste their money. They call *baale shem* for him, or wizards, because they say, 'When the *baal shem tov* or the wizard comes, [it will be driven out].'"

For the most part, Hurwitz tells us, the person becomes even worse. Then the relatives light grass fires to drive out the evil spirits. Finally, the family gives up. The sick man is shown no sympathy, and at last he dies.

> This is a terrible thing, to oppress people who are in the dark without the light of reason, for
> many die because of such worthless healers. But, as I have said to myself, it is those healers
> that harm and destroy the Jewish people. For that wizard, or *baal shem tov* too, is the one
> who causes [the patient] an early death. . . . The patient should be brought to a doctor who
> really knows illnesses and who knows medicine that can cure illness.

After adding further assurances that the patients are really cured in this way, Hurwitz says, "There are those who are truly invaded by an evil spirit or evil dybbuk which is destructive. But this is infrequent, one out of a thousand. This man really needs a *baal shem tov*. Indeed the latter too is rare. One out of a thousand [is genuine]." Hurwitz presents a test for deciding whether the patient has really been invaded by an evil spirit. If the patient reveals secrets about matters of which he was previously ignorant, or speaks a language he never knew, or tells of hidden things which are being done someplace else and turns out to be right, and yet one sees in him foolishness, abnormal actions,

> This is the one who should be taken to a *baal shem tov,* an approved healer, and [given] an
> approved amulet. Undoubtedly, an evil spirit drives him. When to this poor, broken person
> there comes a *baal shem tov* who is God-fearing and who knows the holy names, then he
> will drive out [the evil spirit] from him. But if he does not reveal profound secrets but simply
> says alarming things and does strange things, then he needs a physician like any sick person.

It is also possible to have a good spirit invade one, and this is the holy spirit.

Hurwitz's discussion of "mental health" is of importance for a number of reasons. It distinguishes between physically derived mental illnesses and purely psychological states. But even more important for our purposes is the doubt it casts upon the whole institution of the *baal shem tov,* its view that a genuine *baal shem tov* is very rare. And Hurwitz sees this rare, genuine *baal shem tov* as a mental healer—and a mental healer only.

Furthermore, he rejects such folk practices as the use of smoke to drive out evil spirits, but he accepts the use of amulets. Here he reveals an approach that is generally characteristic of him. The determining factor is Kabbalah. To a twentieth century modern both may appear equally superstitious. But to Hurwitz the validity of a practice is determined by whether it has kabbalistic foundations. Since the use of amulets was authentically kabbalistic, he accepted it.

Hurwitz rejects philosophy and turns to faith.

He judges faith to be superior to reason because the life of the man of faith is superior to the live of the man of reason. But this is not enough for Hurwitz. He also shows that the Jewish life of the Jewish philosophers becomes attenuated, that they give up the mitzvot and so on. Here his analysis is pragmatic.

He next turns to a more philosophic rejection of philosophy. He praises Kant. He quotes at some length Kant's challenge of the accomplishments of metaphysics and Kant's analysis of the antinomies of reason. For Hurwitz, these show the meaninglessness of the philosophic enterprise and the necessity of faith.

He views faith as what man knows and has decided upon in his heart and has formed in his imagination, as something that actually exists; yet it is something which man does not know by demonstration or through the senses. "It is what one knows by tradition, which one receives from one's ancestors or teachers, that such and such actually is real. The heart causes him to believe that completely."

Having surveyed some of the major premises, assumptions, and concerns of the *Book of the Covenant,* we are now in a position to address ourselves to this question: What is the aim of the work?

It is not simply to bring science and liberal ethics to the masses. Despite its European biases, the *Book of the Covenant* is not a kind of prolegomenon on how to be a good eighteenth century European written for the ghetto Jew. Despite its Enlightenment trappings, it is not an Enlightenment book.

The avowed aim of the *Book of the Covenant* is to enable its serious reader to achieve the holy spirit. Phineas Elijah Hurwitz sees himself as no more than a commentator on Hayim Vital's *Gates of Holiness* and Isaac Luria's *Tree of Life,* two sixteenth century mystical works. Vital's introduction to the *Gates of Holiness* discusses the possibility of achieving the holy spirit "even in the present time," and Hurwitz sees his task simply as one of "opening" the gates of the *Gates of Holiness.* He admits that the *Book of the Covenant* is not simply a commentary to the *Gates of Holiness,* but "through the words of my book the words of that book will be understood." Phineas Elijah Hurwitz, then, was an eighteenth century Kabbalist, a disciple of the Luria-Vital school, and that fact contains a whole series of implications which we must explore.

Actually, Hurwitz contributes no new kabbalistic ideas or concepts in this work. He sees himself as a disciple of Luria and Vital, an interpreter of their works.

So, too, Hurwitz achieves nothing in the realm of science. He sees himself as a disciple of modern science, a popularizer.

Hurwitz's originality lies in his attempt to synthesize the two disciplines of science and Kabbalah as the way to acquire the holy spirit. Every Kabbalist assumed that Kabbalah was the way to the holy spirit. But Hurwitz's originality lay in his belief that scientific knowledge was part of this way.

First of all, scientific knowledge is of value for the pious man aside from its help in acquiring the holy spirit. There is a certain grandeur to the universe that one learns about through scientific knowledge. And this grandeur makes one aware of God as the Supernal Sage—a designation that Hurwitz uses frequently. Even man's inventions and achievements, his techniques and explorations, call attention to God's greatness. We come close to the heart of the matter in his discussion of anatomy. Anatomy is important because

> it is closer to the wisdom of Kabbalah than are all the other wisdoms; for God made Man, and it is said, "Then with my flesh will I see God" [Job 19:26]. And it enables one to make an analogy from it [i.e., anatomy] to the spiritual limbs and veins. Furthermore, the [kabbalistic] sages and the enlightened will understand on the basis of this, the construction of the tabernacle, many secrets of the Torah, and the secrets of the upper world.

Hurwitz then proceeds to categorize the parallels between the body organs and the tabernacle (e.g., the heart is in the shape of the ark).

This kabbalistic view of anatomy is made clearer for the modern reader by an observation of Gershom Scholem which is all the more relevant because it deals with Luria, for Hurwitz saw himself as a follower of Luria:

> The structure of Luria's anthropology corresponds on the whole to that of his theology and cosmology, with the difference that the point of reference is no longer the mystical light of divine emanation and manifestation but the soul and its "sparks." Man as he was before his fall is conceived as a cosmic being which contains the whole world in itself and whose station is superior even to that of Metatron, the first of the angels. *Adam ha-Rishon*, the Adam of the Bible, corresponds on the anthropological plane to *Adam Kadmon*, the ontological primary man. Evidently the human and mystical man are closely related to each other; their structure is the same, and to use Vital's own words, the one is the clothing and veil of the other. Here we have also the explanation for the connection between man's fall and the cosmic process, between morality and physics. Since Adam was truly, and not merely metaphorically, all embracing, his fall was bound likewise to drag down and affect everything, not merely metaphorically but really.

The connection, then, between morality and physics (to use Scholem's terms) or the interconnections among science, ethics, and Kabbalah (to use our own terms), which are of fundamental importance for Hurwitz, derive not from Enlightenment premises but from Lurianic premises. These Lurianic premises were no doubt profoundly enriched by Hurwitz's scientific reading, which really could not have been done before the eighteenth century. Hurwitz himself was very much aware of cumulative knowledge, but the driving force of his thought is not the Enlightenment but Lurianic Kabbalah. Thus Hurwitz attaches great importance to the study of man in all his activities; for, as Scholem says, "When he fell into sin, then and then only did this world, too, fall from its former place. . . . Thus there came into being the material world in which we live, and the existence of man as part spiritual, part material, being."

The *Book of the Covenant,* then, is a specifically eighteenth century work in the sense that it depends on eighteenth century popular science, but it is not an Enlightenment work. It is a kabbalistic work, a rather vast addendum to Luria-Vital.

The historic *Sitz-im-leben* of *Sefer Habrith* remains to be plotted. We first turn to the ultimate issues which are considered in the book itself.

What does it mean "to acquire the holy spirit"? First of all, prophecy and the holy spirit are interrelated. The acquiring of either is prevented by any of the following: the violation of a positive or negative commandment, sinful thoughts, sadness, lust, prohibited things, and arrogance. "So as to be included among the wise and the authors of his generation, one must acquire a good character, one must practice good deeds." In addition, as a prerequisite for the acquisition of prophecy and the holy spirit, one must acquire as much wisdom as possible. These are but first steps, however, to acquiring the holy spirit. A person must also repent of his earlier sins, don white clothes, live in complete solitude, meditate past the hour of midnight, reject all imaginations that are involved with the corporeal, contemplate the gradations of the roots of his soul which reach to the very upper worlds, formulate for himself the idea of his ascension to those worlds, and picture to himself the lights that are there. "Eventually, the root of his soul will . . . ascend to the very *en sof.*" Hurwitz here presents a schema of ascent and of the returning descent into the realm of the ordinary world.

There are five degrees of the holy spirit: (1) the dream in which is seen the future, wisdom, and secrets; (2) an angel created through the study of Torah and performance of the mitzvot; (3) an ascension to the very roots of one's soul at the very height of the spheres, which is the complete holy spirit; (4) revelation of Elijah, which comes through piety and separation in which one receives secrets and hidden things of Torah according to the extent of one's piety; and (5) revelation of the souls of the early saints, whether one's soul is involved with them or not. These saints can reveal more secrets of the Torah than any other channel of the holy spirit.

The man who has the holy spirit can acquire secret knowledge and knowledge of the future in various ways. He can understand the speech of birds and other creatures that do not know what they say. For him, even the play of children implies serious things.

A person must do the following things in preparation for acquiring the holy spirit: (1) repent fully; (2) observe the mitzvot meticulously; (3) recite all prayers with intent; (4) study Torah for its own sake; (5) engage in midnight mourning for Jerusalem; (6) diminish one's pleasures; (7) rid oneself of evil characteristics; (8) immerse oneself in water frequently; (9) be as solitary as possible; (10) keep God's name before one's eyes continuously; and (11) cleave with great love to God continuously in one's thoughts.

Once these things have been done, the person should confess, immerse himself, and be alone in an absolutely quiet house. It is better to light it up and be there past midnight; but if he is there during the day, it should be before midday. He should be wrapped in tallith and phylacteries, his eyes closed, and his thoughts so far removed from worldly matters that it is as if he were no longer in this world. With much zeal he should sing a song of praise to God and then direct his thoughts to the higher worlds.

Hurwitz then presents a schema of kabbalistic contemplation. Even if the person does not know the special prayers, he should contemplate. "If you have done all that has been said so as to know whether it will be demonstrated to you and yet you do not feel anything, know of a certainty that you are not yet ready for it." He must continue to do these things if he has not succeeded at the first or second attempt.

The phrase "you do not feel anything" is repeated twice. Feeling is the ultimate test of whether the holy spirit has descended upon one. But what does one feel? The only indication is in the phrase "a spirit will come to one from on high," which indicates an experience of charisma. This phrase is used, however, to introduce the problem of the nature of the spirit which comes, for it may be the spirit of the Evil One. The way to judge is from its message. Is the message completely true or only partly so? Does it contain any foolishness? Does it deny anything in the written or oral Torah?

Evidently, then, receiving the holy spirit is not just a charismatic experience: it also has content. Hurwitz's extended discussion makes this clearer. At first, he says, one achieves minor things, at infrequent intervals. But the more one practices the spiritual exercises he outlines, the greater will be the emanations of the holy spirit, so that they may even come close to prophecy.

And yet this experience must be justified by something beyond itself. Its justification is its purifying quality for character, for good deeds according to Torah, and for the implanting "of the perfect faith in one's heart, as we received it from our ancestors, so that no idea from among the ideas of the philosophers will be mixed up with it." This is the ultimate purpose of the experience: the certitude of a purified, authentically ancestral faith, untainted by philosophy.

The question we must now face is: What is the role of scientific knowledge in acquiring the holy spirit? What part does knowledge of such things as thermometers, sleeping bags, and animal habits play in this process? Hurwitz spent a lot of time acquiring a great deal of "scientific" knowledge. What did it all mean for those who wished to acquire the holy spirit? This is the heart of our problem.

It is worth noting here that there is absolutely no overt mention of Hasidism or the Baal Shem Tov in Hurwitz's very long book. The Gaon of Wilna is mentioned; Mendelssohn is mentioned; Sabbatai Zevi and the Sabbatean movement are mentioned; Jacob Frank is mentioned. Some space is even devoted to Indian Jewry. But the rise of Hasidism, a most important internal event for East European Jewry, is not mentioned.

Had Hurwitz taken Hasidism seriously, he would surely have referred to the

Baal Shem Tov in his discussion of the institution of the *baal shem tov*. His silence at that point suggests a rejection of the entire Hasidic movement.

Hurwitz's techniques for acquiring the holy spirit originate in the earlier kabbalistic tradition. The noisy conventicle centered on the master is absent here. In the *Book of the Covenant* there is no master and no conventicle. There is only the solitary man in a perfectly quiet house.

Phineas Elijah Hurwitz is a Kabbalist, an aristocratic Kabbalist, a disciple of the Luria-Vital school of Kabbalah. His Kabbalism disdains the eighteenth century Hasidic embodiment of Kabbalism. That is why science is so important for Hurwitz. He sees science not as the road to secular enlightenment but as the road to kabbalistic enlightenment.

This view of science clarifies two otherwise unresolved problems of Hurwitz's book. First, there is the strange contradiction, which pervades the *Book of the Covenant* in various ways, between Hurwitz's involvement with science and his acceptance of such things as evil spirits and pre-Copernican astronomy. Hurwitz would seem to be a man who is caught between the medieval and modern worlds. He favors smallpox inoculation, yet he quotes the thirteenth century *Sefer Hasidim* to prove that there are demons. But Hurwitz does not see this as a contradiction. His ultimate criterion is Kabbalah. Therefore, he accepts whatever science denies but Luria-Vital Kabbalah holds as true.

Second, and this is the major problem, Hurwitz never makes explicit the function of scientific knowledge for acquiring the holy spirit. But this becomes clear when we realize that science can lead to the acquisition of the holy spirit if we understand science as being involved with Kabbalah on Hurwitz's terms. Science can awaken the Jew from his "dogmatic slumber"; it can free him from the dangers of Hasidism; it opens the possibility of a return to Luria-Vital Kabbalah. In this sense, science and Kabbalah are partners. But science, of course, is the junior partner. Science is the servant of man. Man is the creator of science. All of this is implied by Hurwitz.

Man, for Hurwitz, is best understood, everything for him is best understood, by Kabbalah. By implication, therefore, science is a servant of Kabbalah. Science is not a specific technique for acquiring the holy spirit. Science simply frees one from provincialism, gives one a picture of the real world. In this world the Jew, without conventicle, without master, can quest for the holy spirit.

Yet there is a master. In fact there are two: Luria and Vital. Their words instruct; and on occasion these masters reveal themselves and secrets of Torah.

The strange quality of the *Book of the Covenant*, its appeal to both the enlightened Jew and the traditional Jew, is thereby clarified. Because of the value it attaches to science and because of its high sense of individuality— its emphasis on the individual in isolation questing for the holy spirit, the religious experience—it is modern in spirit. Because of its kabbalistic orientation, on the other hand, it appeals to the traditional Jew. And because of its kabbalistic orientation the exoteric world of natural phenomena and the esoteric world of Torah secrets, revelations from the holy spirit, and demons are to be found in this book.

The *Book of the Covenant* can be best understood by attending to the following clues to Hurwitz's mind. For Hurwitz, the most important works are Luria's *Tree of Life* and Vital's *Gates of Holiness*, and the ultimate purpose of his book is to provide instruction on how to acquire the holy spirit. An equally important clue to Hurwitz's mind is the fact that he spent his early youth in Galicia and that he actually began the *Book of the Covenant* in Buczacz. Although this fact has been noted by others, its connection with the content of his work has been completely overlooked. Although its significance will not be *proved* by us, for detailed information is unavailable, we consider it highly suggestive. It fits the *Book of the Covenant* into a niche that makes sense of the work, clarifying its ambiguities.

The youthful years spent in Galicia, the book begun in Buczacz, recall Gershom Scholem's discussion of the collapse of Sabbatianism and the possible "ways left open to the Kabbalah." The way of pretending that nothing had really happened rang hollow, says Scholem. Then there was the way of Hasidism, which Scholem plots in the last chapter of *Major Trends in Jewish Mysticism*. But Scholem also mentions another way:

> To renounce all attempts to create a mass movement, in order to avoid a repetition of the disastrous consequences which had followed the most recent of these attempts. That was the attitude of some of the most important representatives of later Kabbalism who entirely renounced the more popular aspects of Lurianism and tried to lead the Kabbalah back from the market place to the solitude of the mystic's semi-monastic cell. In Poland, and in particular in those regions where Sabbatianism and Hasidisim were at home, a spiritual center was once more formed about the middle of the eighteenth century which came to exercise a strong authority, particularly between 1750 and 1800 in Galicia. Here an orthodox anti-Sabbatian Kabbalism flourished and found enthusiastic followers. This was the great age of the *Klaus*, the "close," in Brody. . . . The "close" of Brody, as Aaron Marcus has put it, formed a sort of "paradisical hot-house in which the 'Tree of Life' [as the Lurianic *magnum opus* was called] blossomed out and brought forth fruit."

We believe that this alternative explains Hurwitz's *Book of the Covenant*. It is an alternative which opposes the way of Hasidism. For it "renounces all attempts to create a mass movement. It tries to lead the Kabbalah back from the market place to the solitude of the mystic's semi-monastic cell." Lurianic throughout, it is involved with no "popular aspects of Lurianism." The *Tree of Life*, to which Hurwitz is so deeply committed, is no popular treatise.

Although we have no information which would indicate that Hurwitz either lived in Brody or was involved with the "close" of Brody, we do know that the *Book of the Covenant* was begun in the 1780s in Buczacz, which is in Galicia. And it was in Galicia between 1750 and 1800 that the *"Tree of Life* blossomed and brought forth fruit." Thus we may conclude that the *Book of the Covenant* is a fruit of the "paradisical hot-house" which flourished in Galicia in the second half of the eighteenth century.

But if this is so, yet another paradox confronts us: the great popularity of a work with such aristocratic antecedents. Yet perhaps the seemingly paradoxical popularity of the *Book of the Covenant* may indicate that it remained true to its aim. For with its aristocratic kabbalistic premises it appealed to the individual as individual, and this may have enabled it to cross all ideological lines. Thus its high sense of individualism, that is, its aristocratic bias, may have been one of the basic reasons for its popularity.

There remains yet another question that cannot be avoided, tentative and uncertain though our answer must be: Did Phineas Elijah Hurwitz acquire the holy spirit, whose elicitation is the fundamental concern of his book?

Nowhere in the book does he give us an explicit answer to this most tantalizing question. But an author who with a great certainty imparts to others the techniques of acquiring the holy spirit also seems to be implying that he has applied them successfully himself.

This, at least to us, seems to be implied throughout the book. As we have noted before, this book reflects the optimism of a man who knows what he is about, a man who possesses a cheerful alertness to what is going on in the wider world. We would suggest that these characteristics indicate that the author succeeded in his enterprise. To us they imply that Hurwitz did experience the holy spirit. But, quite correctly from his point of view, he does not say so: first, because, as he indicates, one must not boast of one's accomplishments; and second, and perhaps the two reasons are interrelated, because he is faithful to the Jewish tradition of mystical experience. Gershom Scholem tells us of "the striking restraint observed by the Kabbalists in referring to the supreme experience." In contrast to the mystics who unveiled themselves in autobiographies, "the Kabbalists . . . are no friends of mystical autobiography. . . . They glory in objective description and are deeply averse to letting their own personalities intrude into the picture."

We believe, then, that Hurwitz succeeded in acquiring the holy spirit. He was ultimately a Kabbalist, though not, at least as far as can be judged from the *Book of the Covenant,* a systematic, original theoretician of Kabbalah. But he was truly original in his attempt to weld the new Western science to aristocratic Lurianic Kabbalah. In the *Book of the Covenant* he pursues the old kabbalistic quest for harmony in a new way—that is, he seeks to establish the harmony between the "sphere" of science and the "sphere" of Kabbalah. And in a truly Lurianic way, which was not the way of the Enlightenment, he finds the converging point between the two spheres in the study of man.

The Holy Land and
the American Jew, 1773–1893

Abraham J. Karp

University of Rochester

For the first fifteen centuries of their national existence, the Jewish people lived in the Holy Land.

For the following twenty centuries, the Holy Land lived in the Jewish people— in their memories, in their prayers, in their dreams and aspirations—in all the lands of their dispersal.

What was true in the Old World was equally true in the New. From their earliest days, the Holy Land was part of the most cherished memories and the most fervent hopes of American Jews.

Six documents[1] afford the reader the opportunity of reexperiencing the importance of the Holy Land in the life of American Jews in the course of a biblical life span of 120 years: 1773–1893. The documents illustrate a half-dozen incidents which took place in Newport, New York, Jerusalem, New Orleans, Sacramento, and Pittsburgh.

A Sermon in Newport

May 28, 1773, was a very special day for the Jewish community of Newport, Rhode Island. On this first day of Shavuot, some one hundred men, women, and children had gathered in its beautiful synagogue for worship. Present in the synagogue, among other dignitaries, were Governor Wantan and Justices Oliver and Auchmuty of the Supreme Court of Rhode Island. Observing and recording the event was the Reverend Ezra Stiles, then minister of the Second Congregational Church, later president of Yale.

What had brought the dignitaries to the synagogue was the presence of Rabbi Haijm Isaac Karigal, "Of the City of Hebron, near Jerusalem in the Holy Land." Rabbi Karigal, a native of Hebron, was an emissary of its Jewish community traveling the world over to collect funds. Now on his second trip to the New World, he had spent a month in Philadelphia and five and a half months in New York before coming to Newport.[2]

Ezra Stiles kept a voluminous diary. He noted the visits to Newport of at least six rabbis between 1759 and 1775. Rabbi Karigal impressed him most. The two spent time together in Stiles's study, discussing the Hebrew language, the Bible, the Messiah, and the Holy Land. The majestic, exotic figure of the Holy Land patriarch impressed him so much that he even recorded Rabbi Karigal's attire on the Passover.

> The Rabbi's dress or Apparel: Common English Shoes, black leather Silver Buckles, White Stockings. His general habit was Turkish. A green silk vest. . . . A girdle or sash of colors red and green girt the vest around his Body. . . . When he came into the synagogue he put over all, the usual *Alb* or white *Surplice,* which was like other Jews, except that its Edge was striped with *Blue Straiks,* and had more *fringe.* He had a white cravat around his neck. . . . On his Head a high fur (Sable) cap, exactly like a woman's muff, about 9 or 10 inches high.[3]

The sermon preached by Rabbi Karigal lasted forty-seven minutes and was delivered in "Spanish" (or Ladino). Few understood it, but all were impressed. For that brief time, all of his auditors, Jews and Christians alike, were transported from a seaport town in the New World to the City of the Patriarchs in the Holy Land.

It was not lost on the twenty-five families who formed the Jewish community of Newport that this representative of the Holy Land had brought into their synagogue the leading dignitaries of their province. The Holy Land was sanctified by historic memories that were dear to both the Jews and their Christian neighbors. The presence of this emissary from the Holy Land made them all residents in spirit of the land of the patriarchs and the prophets.

For the Jews of Newport this must have been an exhilarating experience. It lifted a small group of immigrant merchants to the status of scions of an ancient noble tradition wrought by their ancestors—patriarchs, prophets, and kings—in the land chosen by God for His people.

It was a moment that demanded preservation for posterity. Abraham Lopez, a native of Portugal and a former Marrano who six years earlier had entered the covenant of Abraham, was entrusted with the task of translating the sermon into English. This was done after Karigal had left Newport, for he "would *not* consent that it be published."

Published it was, the first Jewish sermon published in America. Writ large on the title page of the sermon is the record of the event and its author, "the venerable Hocham, the Learned Rabbi, Haijm Isaac Karigal," and of what gave the author distinction in the eyes of the whole community of Newport: *"Of the City of Hebron, near Jerusalem in the Holy Land."*

From Ararat to Zion

No American Jew of the nineteenth century was more *the American* than Mordecai Manuel Noah. Born in 1785 of an Ashkenazic father and a Sephardic mother, he spent his early years in Philadelphia and Charleston, finally settling in New York. There he became a leading figure in the city's political and cultural life. He was a newspaper editor, a playwright, and an essayist. A Tammany leader, he held public office as United States consul in Tunis, sheriff of New York, surveyor of the Port of New York, and associate judge of the court of sessions.

His Jewish commitments were equally intense. Noah was a leading member of congregation Shearith Israel and a founder of New York's second congregation, B'nai Jeshurun. He wrote widely on Jewish subjects in the general press and in Jewish periodicals, and he was active in almost every important American Jewish organization and institution of his time.

Rooted though Noah was in the American scene, in American cultural and political life, he maintained an abiding interest in the reconstitution of Jewish statehood. As early as 1818, in the principal address at the dedication of the new synagogue of Congregation Shearith Israel, his most impassioned remarks were reserved for the theme which became his obsession, "the restoration of the Jewish nation to their ancient rights and dominion." His enthusiasm for that restoration raised him to high eloquence:

> They will march in triumphant numbers, and possess themselves once more of Syria, and take their rank among the governments of the earth. . . . Let us then hope that the day is not far distant when . . . we may look forward toward that country where our people have established a mild, just and honorable government, accredited by the world, and admired by all good men.[4]

Noah soon realized that that day would be "far distant." In the meantime, why not create a temporary Jewish commonwealth in the New World—an "asylum," "a city of refuge"? In 1820 he petitioned the New York State legislature to sell him Grand Island, near Buffalo, for that purpose. Five years later he persuaded friends to purchase a section of the island. In an imposing, theatrical dedication, with Noah himself at center stage as self-proclaimed "Judge in Israel," he issued a *Proclamation to the Jews,*[5] inviting the young to come and settle and the others to give monetary support to the enterprise. Noah saw the proposed state, which he named Ararat, as a "city of refuge . . . where our people may so familiarize themselves with the science of government . . . as may qualify them for their great and final restoration to their ancient heritage."[6]

Ararat did not get beyond its dedication. All that remains is the written account which Noah sent to newspapers in America and Europe and the cornerstone now ensconced in the Museum of the City of Buffalo. But in the *root* idea of a Jewish state Noah persisted.

In 1837, in a *Discourse on the Evidences of the American Indians Being the Descendants of the Lost Tribes of Israel,* Noah returned to the dream and certainty of the restoration.

> The Jewish people must now do something for themselves. . . . Syria will revert to the Jewish nation by *purchase.* . . . under the cooperation and protection of England and France, this re-occupation of Syria . . . is at once reasonable and practical.[7]

Seven years later, the return to Zion became the subject of a *Discourse on the Restoration of the Jews,* delivered by Noah at the Tabernacle in New York City on October 28, 1844, and again on December 2. It was published early in 1845.[8] To a largely Christian audience, Noah proclaimed:

> I confidently believe in the restoration of the Jews . . . and believing that political events are daily assuming a shape which may finally lead to that great advent, I considered it a duty to call upon the fine people of this country to aid us in any efforts which, in our present position, it may be prudent to adopt.[9]

The viewpoint Noah put forward and the proposals he made were forerunners of the classic Zionist assertions of later generations. Some of his arguments follow:

1. *Geopolitical considerations:* "Within the last twenty-five years great revolutions have occurred in the East."[10]
2. *The adequacy of Jewish ability to the task:* "The Jews are in a most favorable position to repossess themselves of the promised land, and organize a free and liberal government."[11]
3. *The necessity of Palestine:* "Every attempt to colonize Jews in other countries has failed."[12]
4. *A practical step-by-step program:* "The first step is to solicit from the Sultan of Turkey permission for the Jews to purchase and hold land."[13]
5. *The provision of special aid:* "Those who desire to reside in the Holy Land and have not the means, may be aided by . . . societies to reach their desired haven of repose."[14]
6. *A practical vision:* "Ports of the Mediterranean [will be] occupied by enterprising Jews. The valley of the Jordan will be filled by agriculturists from . . . Germany, Poland and Russia."[15]
7. *The special role of America:* "The liberty and independence of the Jewish nation may grow out of a single effort which this country may make in their behalf. . . . they want only PROTECTION, and the work is accomplished."[16]

In response to criticism of his vision and challenge, Noah wrote: "We in this generation may be impelled to commence the good work, which succeeding generations will accomplish."[17] He wrote this a half century before Theodor Herzl wrote *Der Judenstaat* and 101 years before the establishment of the state of Israel.

The Zionism of Warder Cresson[18]

On November 8, 1860, William R. Page, the United States consul in Jerusalem, informed the secretary of state: "On 27th October last, Warder Cresson, a citizen of the United States, formerly a resident of Philadelphia, died in this city at the age of 62 years."[19]

From the records of the Jewish community of Jerusalem, we learn that Cresson was buried on the Mount of Olives, with honors generally accorded to a prominent rabbi, and that he left behind a wife, the former Rachel Moleano, and two children, David Ben Zion and Abigail Ruth.

An unlikely name, Warder Cresson, for a member of Jerusalem's Sephardic community, and an unlikely nativity as well—American and Christian.

Warder Cresson was born in 1798 to an old and wealthy Quaker family in Philadelphia. A lifelong religious seeker, during his long search he became, in turn, a Quaker, a Shaker, a Mormon, a Millerite, a Hicksite, an Irvingite, a Campbellite—and, in the end, an Israelite.

His religious zeal urged him on to the Holy Land, "to convert Jews and Mohammedans." To do so in style and with authority, he managed to have himself appointed the first American consul in Jerusalem. As soon as the authorities learned of his manner and purpose, the appointment was rescinded; but Cresson was already on his way.

Jerusalem and the Holy Land had a transforming effect on this zealous Christian. He evinced an early interest in the restoration of the Jews to their homeland. At about the same time as Mordecai Manuel Noah was proclaiming his views on the restoration in New York, Cresson in Jerusalem demanded an interview with the pasha, to announce that Scripture had informed him that "the Five Powers and America are about to intervene in Syrian affairs, and the infallible return of the Jews to Palestine."[20]

Within a year, Cresson already felt himself to be more a Jew than a Christian. But as he wrote: "I remained in Jerusalem in my former faith until the 28th day of March, 1848, . . . I was circumcised, entered the Holy Covenant, and became a Jew."[21]

Having become a Jew, Cresson decided to settle in Jerusalem permanently. On September 20, 1848, he returned to Philadelphia to settle his affairs and "make aliyah." His family, now turned Episcopalian, was so outraged at his conversion that his wife and son obtained an "Inquisition of Lunacy" against him and had him declared insane. Following an appeal, he was granted a new trial. The trial, at which some hundred witnesses were called, was a sensation of the day and one of the significant landmarks in America's progress toward religious equality under law. The jury returned a verdict for the defendant, which the press hailed as affirming the "principle, that a man's religious opinions can never be made a test of his sanity."

Cresson remained in Philadelphia for four years, an observant Jew active in Jewish communal and religious life. As a Jew now, calling himself Michael Boaz Israel, he felt drawn again to the Holy Land. In 1852, having published a strange, polemical, autobiographical volume, *The Key of David* (which the family attempted to suppress and destroy), he decided to return to Palestine to "open . . . an extensive farm outside of Jerusalem in the valley of Rephaim."

On the way to Palestine, he published in London a *Circular Letter,* urging a twofold program to aid the Jewish residents of the Holy Land. As an immediate short-range act of philanthropy, he proposed the establishment of a "Soup-House" in Jerusalem. As a long-range practical enterprise, he proposed to set up a "model farm in the valley of Rephaim, to introduce an improved system of English and American farming in Palestine." He challenged: "Will Israel adopt this only true system of *encouraging* practical industry in Palestine, by introducing Agriculture among the Jews, or will we willingly go to ten times the expense . . . to support messenger after messenger every year . . . ?''[22]

On his arrival in Jerusalem, Cresson attempted to establish his model farm. But the noble experiment foundered on the twin rocks of insufficient aid from abroad and lack of interest on the spot. As an American citizen, Cresson solicited ''the protection of the President and government of the United States of America, especially during our infancy; and there is no doubt but that we would succeed in our all-important undertaking.''[23] But the United States government was no more responsive than the Jewish magnates.

Warder Cresson, now Michael Boaz Israel, remained in Jerusalem until his death. He became a full-fledged and honored member of the Sephardic community, serving for a time as its head.

In the pages of the Philadelphia Jewish periodical the *Occident,* Cresson published articles expounding a proto-Zionism which presaged major emphases of classical Zionism:

> The debilitating power of the Diaspora and the revitalizing force of the Holy Land.
>
> Agriculture as the vocation of Israel.
>
> The work of restoration as aiding the coming of the Messiah.
>
> The religion of labor on the soil of the Holy Land.

Cresson argued the superiority of agriculture over manufacturing, urging careful consideration of ''the very great difference there is between the moral tendency, or between the moral and physical health of those educated and brought up in large manufacturing districts, and those brought up in agricultural pursuits.''[24]

In 1856, when Sir Moses Montefiore came to the Holy Land with a bequest of $60,000 from the New Orleans Jewish philanthropist Judah Touro, Cresson urged that the fund be used for agriculture rather than the proposed establishment of a manufacturing training school. It was used for neither, and this bequest brings us to a fascinating document.

Housing in Jerusalem

This writer is a collector of American Judaica and of Hebraica, particularly early Jerusalem imprints. As any collector will tell you, the most satisfying acquisition is one that cuts across more than one field of interest. Five years ago, I found a very rare Jerusalem pamphlet, *Gay Hizayon,* published in 1856. It is a poem in which the secretary of the Ashkenazic community of Jerusalem welcomes Sir Moses and Lady Judith Montefiore to that city. The author, Jacob Saphir, later gained fame for his classic studies on the Jews of Yemen.

Imagine my thrill when I reached stanza 20 on page 12: ''Judah Touro, How lovely your fate!''

And this long footnote:

> This dear person lived in the city of Orleans in America. Before he was called to his eternal reward, he left us as a blessing, from his fortune, $60,000, which amounts to 12,000 pounds sterling, for the residents of Jerusalem and the Holy Land to strengthen their habitation in this land of holiness. He appointed Sir Moses and the purehearted philanthropist Gershom, the son of Israel Dov, called Mr. Kursheedt, to do as they in their wisdom determine. And they have determined to build here a hospital [hospice].

Judah Touro, son of Rabbi Isaac Touro, was the first in a line of American Jewish philanthropists. Born in Newport, Rhode Island, in 1775, he lived most of his life in New Orleans, where he acquired considerable wealth. From time to time he made benefactions to Jewish, Christian, and general charities. His association with Jewish communal and religious life was proper but not intimate. On his death in 1854, his will allotted his considerable fortune to Jewish, Christian, and nonsectarian purposes. Almost all of the Jewish congregations and benevolent societies in America were remembered in it.[25]

Most outstanding, and at the time most noteworthy, was Touro's bequest of $60,000 for the Jews of the Holy Land. Neither time nor space could separate this Jew from the land of his forefathers.

Today Mishkenot Shaananim—the first Jewish housing outside the walls of the old city of Jerusalem—stand as his memorial in Jerusalem. It is ironic, however, that a bequest left for the poor of Jerusalem now benefits some of the city's more affluent citizens and visiting dignitaries, for the area purchased with the Touro bequest is today the site of remodeled dwellings and apartments for visiting writers, scholars, and artists.

A Letter to Sacramento—1860[26]

Judah Touro was, of course, not alone among nineteenth century American Jews for whom the Holy Land was a center of interest and a cause for benevolence. Emissaries from the Holy Land came to the United States in goodly number. They were warmly received and generously supported, as a fine study by Salo and Jeannette Baron indicates.[27] In addition, nationally and locally, Holy Land charity was solicited, collected, and dispensed on an ongoing basis by a network of organizations.

We have mentioned Sir Moses Montefiore, that "uncrowned king" of nineteenth century Jewry. America's Jews used him as their emissary in disbursing their contributions for their brethren in the Holy Land.

Let one document suffice, a letter addressed to:

M. Heyman, Esq.
Sacramento City, California
America

London Grosvenor Gate, Park Lane
29 August 1860

In compliance with your request I forwarded your remittance of £6 for the benefit of the poor in Jerusalem to the Representatives of the different congregations in the Holy City and requested them to acknowledge receipt thereof at their earliest convenience.

I am

Sir

Your obedient servant

Moses Montefiore

Many thousands of miles separated Moses Heyman from the Holy Land, but the brethren there were the concern of a fellow Jew who came up to the goldfields of the Golden Land—and apparently prospered. A Jew in his prosperity did not forget "the poor in Jerusalem." I would argue that the "poor in Jerusalem" aided Heyman more than he aided them. He sent them support for their physical well-being. They, in turn, resident upon the Holy Land, gave him sustenance of spirit, for by being there they made the Holy Land in part also his. They gave Heyman, uprooted from his native land, roots deeper than those he struck in his new home in the New World, roots in a land to which he turned daily in prayer, a land sacred to his ancient people and to his new neighbors as well.

Plan for a State

By vocation, Ralph B. Raphael[28] was a manufacturer of fine hair jewelry. By avocation, he was a writer in the early American Hebrew periodical press. In such periodicals as Zev Schur's *Ha-Pisgah,* he addressed himself to issues of the day, such as those that confronted the East European Jewish community that had been brought to the New World by the oppression and persecution of the Old.

Raphael, a resident of Pittsburgh, Pennsylvania, was an early member of the American *Hovevei Zion* (Lovers of Zion) movement. The movement, though small in number in the 1880s and 1890s, made a significant contribution to Hebrew culture in America, and laid the much-needed foundation for the Zionist activities of the century which followed. The American Lovers of Zion published periodicals and organized the first modern Hebrew schools in America, but the center of their devotion was the growing new yishuv in the Holy Land—pioneers, young and some older, who were founding agricultural colonies in Palestine and who announced themselves as the vanguard of a mass aliyah and a return to the soil of the ancient and now renewed homeland.

In 1893, Raphael published a volume in Hebrew, *She-elat Hayehudim* (The Jewish Question). It is an early Zionist tract worthy of a place in the bibliography of Zionism. In part polemic and in part vision, it argues for a restoration of the Jewish nation to Zion, where alone it can live in peace, security, well-being, and dignity; where alone its spiritual life can be renewed and enhanced.

He levels criticism against the Orthodox,[29] who are so caught up with concern for the minutiae of ritual that they neglect the true life of the spirit; who, waiting for the Messiah, turn away from the great mitzvah of rebuilding and resettling, of living in the Holy Land, the only venue for truly holy living. He turns with even greater scorn upon the Reformers,[30] whose panacea for all the ills that beset the body of Israel is to make cosmetic changes in ritual; who curry the favor of the Gentiles by imitation and assimilation. "Has all this opened for you the doors of their hotels and clubs?" he asks. "Has it lessened their contempt for you?" And, he challenges: Consider what this has done to your own self-respect and dignity. Yet you turn away, he accuses, from the only movement that can give you respect, status, and acceptance among the nations. Nor does he spare the maskilim,[31] the proponents of enlightenment who would have us believe that rich and vibrant cultural life is possible in the Diaspora. And he is, of course, even more scornful of those who urge the gifted young Jews to give their talents to world culture at the expense of their own nation.

He sees only life in the Holy Land as a solution to the endemic anti-Semitism which afflicts the Jewish people even in the enlightened West, even in free, democratic America. He is not unaware of the objections that have been raised to the Zionist dream, and he lists them, eight in number.[32]

Why not settle in the West and in America? Do we dare entrust our lives and substance to the uncivilized tribes who now inhabit the Holy Land—will they not attack the Jewish colonies as they now attack Christian missions? Will the Ottoman Empire accept us and protect us? Can we indeed all settle in a land not large enough to accommodate one-fifth of the Jewish people? Can this land support a population unskilled in agriculture and unfit for manual labor? Will the Christians permit us to settle a land that is holy to them? Will we be able to undertake all the menial tasks that a self-contained community requires? How will we be able to unite a people as divided in views and visions as "the East is distant from the West"?

He is certain that the Jewish people has the capacity to face up to the challenges and solve the problems. As a devout Lover of Zion, he points to the already established agricultural colonies in Palestine, drawing an idyllic, idealized picture of life on the soil, of husband, wife, and children joined together in an enterprise which has transformed their very being, which has straightened their backs and lifted their spirits. He hails the halutzim as the creators of the new Jew and a new society. For such a person and such a society, no problem is too difficult, no challenge too great.

He also points out that the Jews have suffered far more from the civilized Europeans than from the uncultured Asians. Yet it is to the civilized nations that the world looks for a political solution. His vision goes beyond the status of a colony to that of a self-governing nation.

The most fascinating section of the volume is entitled "*Emek Yehoshafat* (The Valley of Jehoshaphat): A Conjecture Only."[33] The title is from Joel 4:1.

> For behold, in those days, and in that time,
> When I shall bring back the captivity of Judah and Jerusalem,
> I will gather all nations,

> And will bring them down into the valley of Jehoshaphat;
> And I will enter into judgment with them there
> For My people and for My heritage Israel,
> Whom they have scattered among the nations,
> And divided My land.

Let us imagine, he proposes, that the idea of resettling the land has won the majority of Jewish hearts and made adherents among the nations, that the Jews of America will buy land for those who want to settle, and that fellow Jews in other countries will join in the enterprise. To the degree that Jews will settle on the land and make it flourish, to that degree will the nations of the world look with favor on the enterprise.

And the nations of the world would appoint a commission of twelve judges who will hear the claims of the contenders for the Holy Land—the Catholics, the Greek Orthodox, the Protestants, the Moslems, and the Jews—and decide: *For whom the Holy Land*.

The trial is held. The representatives of the great faiths make their presentations and pleas.

It will come as no surprise to us to learn that after due deliberation the commission renders the decision: *Palestine is for the Jewish people*.

Above all other considerations, the enterprise and the accomplishment of the Jewish farm colonists will have determined this.

Raphael puts forth his political philosophy in seventeen points which constitute the commission's decision. Among them are:

> The Turkish government is to be sovereign in all external matters.
>
> Christian colonies may remain so long as they do not disturb the peace of the land.
>
> Christian immigration is to be restricted, to be determined by Jews.
>
> A Christian commission is to supervise the holy places.
>
> A special Jewish agency is to be appointed by the nations to facilitate Jewish immigration.
>
> The Jews may organize a militia to keep the peace.
>
> For all internal matters, the Jews are to organize a republican form of government, which is to meet in Jerusalem.
>
> The Jewish government may mint its own coinage, levy taxes, and elect a president who will serve for a five-year term, with the approval of the Turkish government.
>
> The representative body, called the Sanhedria, is to be elected for a ten-year term, and will be empowered to govern.
>
> The president and vice-president and the members of the Sanhedria are to be Jews by birth.
>
> The Turkish government may use the army of the Jews in its warfare.[34]

We note the desire for a fully Jewish state, with autonomy—but Raphael, the realist, recognizes that the Ottoman Empire will retain sovereignty. He could not conceive of sovereignty being purchased or wrested from the "sick man of Europe." To the leading nations of Europe, the Turkish Empire may have looked "sick"; to colonists in Palestine and to a Zionist dreamer in Pittsburgh, it was a mighty power.

Three years later, Theodor Herzl issued his pamphlet *Der Judenstaat.*

It remains now to consider the factor "America" in the Zionism of Mordecai Manuel Noah and Ralph B. Raphael. How did the atmosphere and experience of America help shape their concept and expression of Zionism?

Noah was the product of early nineteenth century America, an America which was experiencing a religious and national awakening. Because it was a young nation, its gaze was turned, as the gaze of the young is apt to be turned, to the future. Religious life was marked by emphasis on Adventism. Second Coming expectations were in the air. For Noah, the American Jew, this took expression in an inordinate interest in messianism, that aspect of the Jewish ethos which has its roots in the past but which places its emphasis on the future. For the nineteenth century American Christian, messianism meant the Second Coming of the Christ. For Noah the Jew it meant the fulfillment of the promised restoration of the Jews to the Holy Land.

"I firmly believe in the restoration of the Jews, and in the coming of the Messiah," Noah proclaimed. "The return of the Jews to Jerusalem, and the organization of a powerful government in Judea [will] lead to that millennium which we all look for, all hope for, all pray for," he told his American Christian audience.[35]

This was a belief and commitment which Jew and Christian shared. Noah the Jew felt so secure in America that he could ask the Christians to participate in the fulfillment of the Jewish Messianic dream.

Added to the Judeo-Christian messianism current in nineteenth century America was the American sense of national mission. America came into being to fulfill a destiny and a mission—a destiny to grow strong and great and a mission to use that strength and greatness in service to other peoples and nations. Noah, the American, could then call upon his fellow Americans:

> Where, I ask, can we commence this great work of regeneration with a better prospect of success than in a free country with a liberal government? Where can we plead the cause of independence for the Children of Israel with greater confidence than the cradle of American liberty? Here we can unfurl the standard and seventeen millions of people [i.e., the American nation] will say, "God is with you; we are with you; in His name and in the name of civil and religious liberty, go forth and repossess the land of your fathers."[36]

He is confident that this will be the response of America to Jewish national aspirations, for "we have advocated the independence of the South American republic. . . . we have combated for the independence of Greece."[37] "If these nations are entitled to our sympathies," he argues, "how much more powerful and irrepressible are the claims of that beloved people" whom God "for their special protection and final restoration had dispersed among the nations of the earth, without confounding them with any!"[38]

Noah, the American Jew, welded the religious messianism and sense of national mission which pervaded his America into his concept of and promotion of the Zionist dream. He was realist enough to recognize that the establishment of a state was a long and laborious process. He asked the aid of his fellow Americans in settling Jews upon their ancient homeland as the first step.

> The appeal I have made . . . places the Jews in the Holy Land as mere proprietors, protected in their possessions as other citizens and subjects—and this is the basis of the restoration. Other events will follow in their proper course.[39]

It may well be that the order of, first, an established community and then a state grew out of Noah's perception of the American experience of "conquest through settlement." Settlement as the base for sovereignty became even more evident in America's expansion westward as area after area settled by Americans became states of the nation.

Erwin Rosenberger, an early co-worker of Theodor Herzl, quotes the founder of political Zionism: "We will do it differently, first the land, then the colonization. First we must be the legal owners of a whole territory; afterwards we can make it arable and build it up."[40]

Raphael, even more strongly than Noah, proposed a reverse order: first colonization, then a state. "In fifty years," he wrote in 1893, "about two million Jews will be settled in the land of their fathers."[41] The community would grow because the colonists now resident there would "extend their hands . . . to receive in love" their brethren, "the despoiled in Morocco, the downtrodden in Yemen, the persecuted in Russia, the oppressed in Persia and the unfortunate in Roumania."[42]

In the trial before the "Tribunal of Nations," the plea of the representatives of the Jewish people would be:

> Permit us then to return to our ancestral homeland, to settle it, to work it—there to serve the Lord our God. Let us reside in the land of our fathers as you reside in the land of yours. . . . We shall be happy in our land as you will be in yours. And slowly but surely, you will begin to accept us as part of the body of humanity.[43]

Raphael bases his certainty about the future on the accomplishments of the present.

> The halutzim have raised the banner of Judah in pride for their persecuted brethren to return to the land of their fathers, to work the land and benefit from its bounties. The pioneers, the Bilu, inspired many of their people with their courage and strength. May their brethren follow in their ways to lay the cornerstone for the rebuilding of the household of Israel in the land of its fathers.[44]

The life of the halutzim upon the land is the most telling statement to the nations:

> I adjure you, worthy judges, in the name of truth and justice, what fault can you find with these good people laboring to establish a homeland; these decent people who are casting off the parasitic existence which you forced upon them. See them take hold of the plow to work the land of their fathers by the sweat of their brow.[45]

The favorable verdict of the tribunal is based entirely on the accomplishment of the pioneer colonists:

> We, the judges appointed by the nations of Europe to judge in righteousness among the parties and faiths, do arrive at the decision: after due and careful consideration of the goals of the colonists who have come to the land of their fathers, . . . settling it to earn their livelihood by the sweat of their brow, . . . we render our decision that *Palestine is for the Jewish People.*[46]

The dual emphases of national existence as mission and settlement as the base for sovereignty are voiced by both Noah and Raphael. Their Zionism was colored by their perception of the developing American nation. For them, the emergence of a Jewish commonwealth would parallel the American experience of nation making. A Jewish nation would be formed by an ingathering of peoples who settled upon the land and wrested its God-given bounties through exertions of hand and mind. In that land the individuality of each group would be merged into a common culture and united by a new vision of statehood—a nation with a mission of service to humanity.

The Zionism of Noah and Raphael was an American Zionism, a Zionism rooted in Jewish messianism and attuned to the needs of the Jewish people, but infused with the American vision of nationhood and inspired by the American experience of nation building.

Time and distance separated the colonial Jewish community of Newport, the New York proto-Zionist, the Philadelphia Quaker turned Jerusalem colonist, the New Orleans philanthropist, the Sacramento contributor, and the Pittsburgh Lover of Zion, but the presence of the Holy Land in their memories, vision, concerns, and aspirations impelled them all to make some contribution to the foundation forged by ideology, commitment, and deeds upon which stands the state of Israel.

NOTES

1. The documents—three pamphlets, two books, and a letter—are:

Haijm Isaac Karigal, *A Sermon Preached at the Synagogue, in Newport, Rhode Island . . .* (Newport, 1773).

M. M. [Mordecai Manuel] Noah, *Discourse on the Restoration of the Jews* (New York, 1845).

Warder Cresson, *The Key of David* (Philadelphia, 1852).

Jacob Saphir, *Gay Hizayon* (Jerusalem, 1855).

Letter, Moses Montefiore to M. Heyman, August 29, 1860.

R. [Ralph] B. Raphael, *She-elat Hayehudim* (n.p., 1893).

2. For Karigal (Raphael Hayyim Isaac Carigal), see *Encyclopedia Judaica,* 5:179–80; and Abraham J. Karp, *Beginnings: Early American Judaica* (Philadelphia, 1975), pp. 11–16.

3. Quoted by Morris Jastrow, Jr., "References to Jews in the Diary of Ezra Stiles," in *The Jewish Experience in America,* ed. A. J. Karp, 1:163–64.

4. Mordecai M. Noah, *Discourse, Delivered at the Consecration of the Synagogue of Congregation*

Shearith Israel in the City of New York (New York, 1818), pp. 27–28. For Noah and Zionism, see Louis Ruchames, "Mordecai Manuel Noah and Early American Zionism," *American Jewish Historical Quarterly* 64, no. 3 (1974–75): 195–223.

5. For the text of the *Proclamation,* see Joseph Y. Blau and Salo W. Baron, *The Jews of the United States, 1790–1840* (New York and London, 1963), pp. 894–905.

6. Ibid., p. 895.

7. M. M. Noah, *Discourse on the Evidences of the American Indians* (New York, 1837), p. 38.

8. See Karp, *Beginnings,* pp. 57–65.

9. Noah, *Discourse,* p. v.

10. Ibid., p. 33.

11. Ibid., p. 35.

12. Ibid.

13. Ibid., p. 37.

14. Ibid., p. 38.

15. Ibid.

16. Ibid., p. 51.

17. *Occident* 3 (1845): 34.

18. See Abraham J. Karp, "The Zionism of Warder Cresson," in *Early History of Zionism in America,* ed. Isadore Meyer (New York, 1958), pp. 1–20.

19. *Diplomatic Dispatches: Jerusalem,* National Archives, Washington, D.C., mss., vol. 1.

20. William M. Thackeray, "Notes of a Journey from Cornhill to Cairo," in *The Works of William Makepeace Thackeray* (New York, 1904), vol. 21, p. 304.

21. Cresson, *Key of David,* p. 205.

22. *Occident* 10 (1852): 609–11.

23. Ibid., 12 (1854): 355.

24. Ibid., 13 (1855): 136.

25. The will is published in Max J. Kohler, "Judah Touro, Merchant and Philanthropist," in *The Jewish Experience in America,* ed. A. J. Karp, 2:169–76.

26. The Montefiore–Heyman letter is in possession of the author. The letter of Moses Heyman to Montefiore accompanying his contribution is in possession of Adolph Schisha, London.

27. Salo W. and Jeannette M. Baron, "Palestinian Messengers in America, 1849–79: A Record of Four Journeys," *Jewish Social Studies* 5 (1943): 115–62, 225–92.

28. For Ralph B. Raphael, see Ida Cohen Selavan, "A Pre-Herzlian Jewish State: Ralph B. Raphael's *She-elat Hayehudim,*" *American Jewish Historical Quarterly* 66, no. 3 (1976–77): 432–35.

29. Raphael, *She-elat Hayehudim,* p. 6 ff.

30. Ibid., p. 19 ff.

31. Ibid., p. 23 ff.

32. Ibid., pp. 26–27.

33. Ibid., p. 74 ff.

34. Ibid., pp. 105–6.

35. Noah, *Discourse,* p. 10.

36. Ibid.

37. Ibid.

38. Ibid., p. 11.

39. Ibid., p. viii.
40. Erwin Rosenberger, *Herzl as I Remember Him* (New York, 1959), p. 17.
41. Raphael, *She-elat Hayehudim*, p. 78.
42. Ibid., p. 79.
43. Ibid., p. 104.
44. Ibid., pp. 103–4.
45. Ibid., p. 104.
46. Ibid., pp. 105–6.

The Social Foundation of Jewish Modernity

Paula Hyman

Columbia University

Jews have often been portrayed as quintessential moderns. Bursting out of their ancient communities with vigor and striding onto the stage of modern history in the nineteenth century, they were blamed for inflicting the evils of the modern world upon tranquil traditional societies. Jews, it was said, were rootless and cosmopolitan, promoters of finance and industrial capitalism, secularization, and liberalism. As one popular German writer, Paul de Lagarde, described them late in the nineteenth century, they were "the carriers of decay [who] pollute every national culture; they exploit the human and material resources of their hosts; they destroy all faith and spread materialism and liberalism."[1] In short, they seemed to thrive under the pressure of the modern world, while other groups wilted under its assault.

Yet Jews were not always seen in this light. At the end of the eighteenth century, when a debate raged about the admissibility of Jews as citizens into civilized European societies, the image of the Jew was far different. Rather than being viewed as a prophet of modernity, the Jew was perceived as clannish, backward, and superstitious, laboring under the burdens of a tradition that was out of step with the requirements of the age. In the words of the Abbé Grégoire, the liberal French cleric who sought the regeneration of the Jews during the French Revolution, they were "attached not only to the Mosaic law, but to superimposed chimeras, in which is expressed a blind credulity."[2]

Cut off from social contact with their countrymen, Jews lived according to their own customs, wore distinctive dress, and pursued a limited range of occupations. So common a sight was the Jewish peddler, hawker of old clothes, horse trader, and money lender that in many places the word *Jew* became virtually synonymous with these trades. As late as 1830, the *Gentleman's Magazine,* published in England, commented that it was difficult "to separate the idea of Jews from peddlers who cry 'old clothes,' hawk sealing wax, and have a peculiar physiognomical character."[3]

How, then, did Jews so quickly become the symbols of modernity? How were they transformed from peddler to Rothschild, from cultural laggard to avant-garde intellectual? How did they come to be so much at home in the urban societies of Europe and America? My purpose in asking these questions is to explore the processes of modernization among Jews in the Western world rather than to date with precision the beginning of the modern period of Jewish history.[4] In doing so, I hope to illuminate both the Jewish experience and the Jewish image of the past two centuries.

Modern societies have generally been characterized by the weakening of a traditionally religious world view and by the substitution of rational criteria for subjective ones in the economic and social spheres. For example, modern industrial societies distribute social and economic roles according to skill achieved rather than by birth. The nation-state centralizes authority and works to destroy and coopt institutions that might compete for the loyalty of the individual citizen. Jewish modernity shares in the larger trends of the modern period—in secularization, urbanization, the rise of individualism, and industrialization. But it has its own particular character as well. For Jews, modernity has meant the breakdown of the rabbinic tradition as the dominant force in Jewish life and the transformation of a compulsory, self-governing, all-embracing community into a voluntaristic one. It has meant civic emancipation as well—the achievement by Jews of the rights and obligations of citizenship in their countries of residence—and the acculturation and social integration which accompanied their new legal status. In addition to these sociocultural and political components, Jewish modernity has an ideological component. It has involved an eagerness to break loose from galut, from exile. What Shabbetai Tzevi, the seventeenth century messianic pretender, Gabriel Riesser, the nineteenth century proponent of civil rights for German Jews, and David Ben-Gurion, the twentieth century Zionist, all had in common was the desire to bring the period of exile to a close: the first by ushering in the messianic age, the second by achieving emancipation and integration wherever Jews lived, and the third by reconstituting an independent Jewish state. In their attitudes toward exile, all three expressed versions of Jewish modernity. For Jews, the modern period has meant changing their very relationship to the world around them.

This transformation of social relations and ideology did not occur simultaneously to all Jews. Geographic and class differences were critical. It was the Jews of Western and Central Europe, as well as the United States, who developed the models of Jewish modernity. The Jews of Eastern Europe did not become modern until late in the nineteenth century or, some would argue, not until after the Russian Revolution, while the Jews of the Near East and North Africa did not confront the modern world until well into the twentieth century. Similarly, it was the Jewish upper and lower classes who first cast off the traditional ways of the Jewish community and sought social contact with their non-Jewish peers. The Jewish lower middle classes held longest to traditional customs and to social aloofness from the Gentile world.

The challenge of modernity was the same throughout the Western world—the need to provide a new rationale for continued Jewish existence and to define the relationship of Jews to the societies in which they lived. However, there were local innovations in the precise formulation of the challenge and in the types of responses which Jews developed. Jewish socialism could emerge only in Eastern Europe, where both ethnic minority nationalism and mass revolutionary movements were strong, while religious reform could take root only in those Western countries, such as Germany and the United States, where liberal Protestantism provided a model. Though I will generalize about the processes of Jewish modernization, it is important to bear in mind that general developments conceal a wealth of specific differences.

Jewish modernity was dependent on a combination of internal factors and impetus from the outside world. Zionist historians have emphasized developments within the Jewish community—in particular, the antinomianism and the antirabbinic attitudes unleashed by the Sabbatian movement. These internal changes predisposed Jews to break with the norms of traditional Judaism and to view the powers of the Jewish community and its leadership as coercive rather than protective. They were important, for they prepared Jews to look to the larger society and to accept emancipation. Yet Zionist historians have paid too little attention to the impact of the larger society. Developments within the Jewish community led to modernity only in those societies which offered new opportunities to Jews and accepted the new concept of equality before the law, that is, in societies which experienced the birth of liberal capitalism. While the Sabbatian movement was strongest in Turkey, for example, Ottoman Jewry did not confront the issues posed by modernity until Turkey itself embarked upon the process of modernization. By holding aloft the potential of meeting Gentiles in what Jacob Katz has called the "semi-neutral society,"[5] Western nations enabled, and encouraged, Jews to entertain the possibility of new professions, new places of residence, and new self-definitions vis-à-vis the outside world. Only when the intellectual, political, and social climate has nurtured the possibility of change can change become a reality.

The beginnings of modernity among Jews can be found in two different types of change—in behavior and in consciousness. Change in behavior, it would seem, occurred first in the West. When small numbers of wealthy Jewish merchants had occasion for economic contacts with Gentiles of their own or of the upper classes in the middle of the seventeenth century, they began to adopt the customs of Gentile society. As historians have pointed out, as early as the first part of the eighteenth century upwardly mobile, socially aspiring German Jews taught French, Italian, and piano to their daughters as a sign of their own high status. Women began to read novels on the Sabbath while their menfolk indulged themselves with card playing. Mixed dancing and promenades appeared as social diversions. The wealthiest of the Jews, and in particular the Court Jews who served the nobility as bankers and army suppliers, patterned their style of dress after their aristocratic patrons.[6] Lower-class Jews, too, often followed the mores of their Gentile peers, especially when Jewish communal constraints were weak. In eighteenth century England, for example, poor Jews engaged in street fighting and pickpocketing. A few even earned fame and fortune in prizefighting, a sport not widely acclaimed by Jewish tradition. In Central Europe as well, lower-class Jewish criminality was not uncommon, as poor Jews mimicked the behavior of the Gentiles with whom they had contact.[7]

By looking to Gentile society for their standards of behavior, Jews were implicitly making a statement about their values. These were no longer to be governed exclusively by the internal norms of traditional Jewish society. That implicit statement was made explicit by the end of the eighteenth century, when a new Jewish elite, the maskilim, consciously referred to external criteria to evaluate Jewish tradition and to legitimate their own activity. The maskilim emerged from upper bourgeois Jewish circles—from the ranks of bankers, wholesale merchants, and industrialists. Even the great philosopher Moses Mendelssohn, the son of a poor Torah scribe from Dessau, was dependent for his livelihood on a wealthy Berlin Jewish silk manufacturer, who employed him as a bookkeeper. In 1774 one Gentile observer described the Berlin maskilim, with some surprise, as "refined and well-bred. Persons of rank among them were consorting much with Christians and participating together with them in innocent amusements, and often it was hard to tell that they were Jews at all."[8]

The maskilim promoted a new set of priorities and a new leadership within the Jewish community. Secular studies, once appreciated only for their contribution to the understanding of Torah, were now to take precedence over traditional Jewish learning. While continuing to use the utilitarian argument that a secular education made one a better Jew, early maskilim like Hartwig Wessely added a new argument—that secular learning was valuable in and of itself. The cultivation of the individual and his talents became a goal equal to that of serving God or the community. Along with their propagation of Gentile culture, the maskilim presented themselves, lay Jewish intellectuals rather than traditionally trained rabbis, as the natural leaders of the Jewish community. Through their writings, their example, and the schools they established, the maskilim influenced several generations of Jewish youth. By the beginning of the nineteenth century, ideology thus served both to justify and to promote aspirations for the political, social, and cultural changes we associate with Jewish modernity.

The majority of Jews, however, were neither maskilim nor their followers. Peddlers and storekeepers of modest means, living in villages and small towns, they followed a far more gradual path of modernization than their more illustrious intellectual and upper middle-class fellow Jews. To them emancipation meant first and foremost the opportunity to make a better living and to relocate to achieve that goal. Both occupational and residential restrictions had characterized Jewish life prior to the French Revolution. In the nineteenth century, Jews could become entrepreneurs and retailers, and most Jews in the West parlayed their traditional economic skills into more prosperous and more prestigious forms of commerce than peddling. Throughout Western and Central Europe, the percentage of Jewish peddlers declined precipitously by mid-century.[9]

And Jews were on the move in large numbers, migrating from one village to another and from village to city. In fact, mass migration (from East to West) may well be the most distinctive and important social phenomenon of the modern Jewish experience. It was migration that often precipitated other aspects of modernization. Migration strains the social fabric, entailing both physical and psychological dislocation. Uprooted from their small traditional communities, the Jews who moved from village to city were freed from the constraints of social disapproval that prevailed in village society. The city offered a measure of social anonymity to its new inhabitants. Often more venturesome than their coreligionists who stayed put, the Jewish migrants may also have been predisposed to innovate in matters of social and religious behavior as well as geographic mobility. It is no accident, then, that religious laxity appeared first and most prominently in England and the United States, the two Western communities which were composed entirely of immigrants from Western and Central Europe. In both countries the control which the community exercised over its members was weak, and abandonment of Hebrew, casualness in the observance of the Sabbath and of kashrut, and even intermarriage were noted by the end of the eighteenth century. If Jewish modernity is measured by a sustained movement of acculturation in speech, dress, and social life, along with a decline in traditional religious practice, then British and American Jewry were the first modern Jewish communities.

My own research on the Jews of Alsace suggests that at least 25 percent of Western Jews, and possibly more, were on the move even in the first half of the nineteenth century.[10] Therefore, the modernizing and disrupting effects of migration should not be minimized. Moreover, rabbis too were no strangers to geographic mobility within Europe. Often university-trained rabbis found their first pulpits in small towns. There they introduced their congregants to innovations in religious practice and stimulated interest in secular learning as well.

Still, as late as the middle of the nineteenth century most of the Jews who lived in rural areas—that is, the majority of both French and German Jews—were still traditional in their religious observance and in their world view. For example, as late as the 1860s, three generations after emancipation, more than half of the civil marriage documents of Alsatian Jews living in villages and towns included signatures in Hebrew characters, indicating that many individuals had mastered neither French nor German. In the same period, young Jewish men in Alsace invoked the aid of Rabbi Meir Baal Haness in a ritual incantation, written in a combination of Yiddish and Hebrew, to secure a high number in the draft lottery, thus exempting them from military service.[11] While assimilation had made significant strides in the cities, even there a sizable number of traditional Jews were still to be found. Only later in the century were the processes of social and economic change among Jews particularly rapid.

Furthermore, Jews have retained many aspects of their premodern existence even in the modern period. Social theorists of modernity expected that all particularism would disappear into a universal culture. The majority of Jews, however, did not abandon Judaism entirely; rather, they modified their observance and attempted to modernize Jewish practice and ideology to provide a rationale for continued Jewish existence. Jewish leaders, Reform and Orthodox alike, redefined Jewish identity in exclusively religious terms. However, they argued that Judaism, properly understood, preserved the essence of monotheism in its purest form and hence had a distinct contribution to make to modern cultures. If Jews began to see themselves as French, German, or American citizens, their new national self-definition did not seem to them to conflict with their Jewish identity or to demand its abandonment. Indeed, Jews in all countries proclaimed the compatibility of Judaism with the national culture. The very survival of a Jewish community, which in parts of Europe was able to tax its members into the twentieth century, is testimony to the desire of Jews to assert a group identity reminiscent of their separatist status in the medieval world. If most Jews modernized gradually and never completely abandoned their premodern attributes, why, then, the image of the Jew as exceptionally modern? The answer lies in the peculiarities of Jewish modernization and in the political history of Jewish emancipation.

Jews were well equipped by their historical experience to adapt to many of the features of modern society. Yet, paradoxically, the psychological process of modernization was particularly difficult and extreme for them.

In economic terms, modernization came easily. Even in the Middle Ages, Jews had engaged in quasi-modern, that is, protocapitalist, occupations. While their involvement with money and commerce had contributed to their stigmatization by medieval Christian culture, in modern times this economic liability became an asset. Jews thought in terms appropriate to capitalist societies and brought with them skills necessary for economic success in the modern world. Their role as moneylenders in credit-starved rural regions provided them with sufficient liquid capital to begin new enterprises or expand old ones. They were used to taking risks, to investing their money, and to participating in a market economy. Moreover, their high rate of literacy was useful in urban societies. Thus, in the course of the nineteenth century they prospered. Even in areas not noted for Jewish wealth, such as Alsace-Lorraine, the majority of Jews improved their economic status. [12]

At the same time, European peasants and artisans found the diffusion of capitalism economically and socially disruptive. Since their traditional methods of marketing and production were no longer competitive, they faced impoverishment and loss of social status. The system that Jews found congenial was therefore threatening to large segments of the Gentile population. The German sociologist

Ferdinand Tönnies aptly summed up the traditionalists' hostility to the triumph of a modern commercial spirit. "The will to enrich himself," he claimed, "makes the merchant . . . the type of egotistic, self-willed individual to whom all human beings, except his nearest friends, are only means . . . to his ends or purposes; he is the embodiment of Gesellschaft."[13] Moreover, the use of money to make money—as in finance capitalism—appeared mysterious and suspicious to much of the general population. Thus, the very success of a few prominent Jewish bankers, such as the Rothschilds, Pereires, and Bleichroders, fed the popular stereotype of the crafty Jew who profited illicitly from devious economic arrangements. Even the socialist leader Jean Jaurès, who was to risk his career in defense of Captain Dreyfus, asserted about Jewish financiers that "their long association with banking and commerce had made them peculiarly adept in the ways of capitalist criminality."[14]

It is no wonder, then, that anti-Jewish riots erupted in both France and Germany during the Revolution of 1848. A group of artisans from Leipzig explained the rationale for anti-Jewish hostility in a proclamation opposing the emancipation of the Jews. "There is no greater enemy of the petty bourgeoisie and of the laboring classes, no greater enemy of the solidity of the small trades than these aliens," they declared of the Jews. "Their heart is the money bag. . . . Usury originates chiefly among [them], and they ruin the handicraft shop with their system of bargaining. . . . We have largely their doing to thank for the growing proletariat, which their orators and writers then incite against the existing order."[15] This perception of the Jew as the agent of capitalism prevailed among the lower middle classes throughout Western and Central Europe, and in the last decades of the nineteenth century it enabled anti-Semitism to become one of the major vehicles for expressing anti-modernist sentiments.[16] If capitalism was the modern economic form par excellence, Jews were considered its standard-bearers.

Furthermore, Jews were not only particularly capable of taking advantage of the economic opportunities offered by capitalism, by virtue of their historical experience and their cultural proclivities. They were also attracted by urban living and migrated to cities in numbers far in excess of their proportion of the general population. Even when they lived in rural areas, Jews had not developed the attachment to the soil characteristic of peasants, and their occupations had been semiurban. Hence, the move to the city was not the trauma for Jews that it was for the displaced peasant recruited into the urban working class. The city offered Jews diverse economic opportunities, particularly in commercial employment, but, at least before the arrival of immigrants from Eastern Europe, it did not create a Jewish industrial working class. Thus, the experience of Jews and Gentiles within the city differed. Moreover, the concentration of Jews within major European cities lent credence to the notion of the city as a Jewish phenomenon. Jews were visible in cities. "Berlin," declared one German writer, "is the domain of the Jews."[17] To those nostalgic for a romanticized version of traditional rural society, the city came to represent the embodiment of the ills of modern life. It was a cold, unhealthful, and cruel environment; it enabled foreigners to perpetuate their peculiar cultures, and dominated by the proletariat and immigrants, it was a breeding ground for political radicalism. Thus, the city undermined healthy nationalism, which was rooted in the soil.

Finally, Jews were seen as radical modernists in both culture and politics. Although Peter Gay has persuasively argued that there were as many cultural conservatives as cultural modernists among Jews,[18] in the popular mind Jews were the incarnation of the modernist critique of bourgeois society. When a Léon Blum attacked the conventional family, advocating premarital sexual experimentation for women as well as men, his views were taken as representative of those held by Jews as a whole. When Georg Simmel, son of Jewish converts, pioneered in the field of sociology, his work was seen as a specifically Jewish attack upon the primacy of the state. Jewish artists, radical Jewish intellectuals, and Jewish scholars in the forefront of new academic disciplines all symbolized the disturbing intellectual ferment that has so often been associated with Jews. Romain Rolland, the French author, succinctly expressed the popular fear of the Jew as eroder of traditional values in the comment that "unfortunately, the past does not exist for the Jews."[19]

On the political front, the participation of Jews in revolutionary movements was also taken as an expression of their resentment of the traditional Christian society from which they had been excluded. Though radical Jews from Karl Marx to Leon Trotsky have been, at best, ambivalent about their Jewishness and, at worst, notorious embodiments of Jewish self-hatred, their very activity labeled all Jews as politically suspect. They were highly visible, articulate proponents of radical change. Though the revolutionary movements would have flourished without them, it was easy, and useful, for the political Right to portray revolution, and even such values as democracy and egalitarianism, as clever Jewish inventions, aimed at the destruction of the societies of Christian Europe.

There was sufficient truth to the popular stereotype to enable it to flourish, particularly since exceptional Jews—the articulate and the prominent—attracted so much public attention that they came to represent all Jews. The rise of new possibilities and social arrangements created by the Enlightenment and by emancipation had of necessity undermined traditional Jewish ways of defining the world. To use the terminology of the prominent sociologist of religion Peter Berger, the "plausibility structure" of traditional Judaism was weakened and then destroyed.[20] That is, the specific community and the social reality which had confirmed the world view of traditional Judaism was transformed. The autonomous Jewish community, the traditions of rabbinic Judaism, and religioethnic self-definition had told Jews who they were, how the world operated, and what the Jews' position in that world was. Now, the Jewish tradition ceased for many to provide a meaningful explanation of the modern Jewish world. With emancipation a reality or a promise, nineteenth century Western Jews—and particularly the intellectuals and the upwardly mobile among them—no longer felt themselves to be in exile. The Gentile world appeared less and less threatening, and its culture highly attractive. Maskilim therefore developed an ideology consonant with a different plausibility structure—one of integration rather than segregation. As Berr Isaac Berr, a French maskil, wrote optimistically of a time when Jewish and Gentile children would study together in school, "Through this union in the schools our children, as well as those of our fellow citizens, will notice from their tender youth that neither difference of opinion nor of religion in any way prevents fraternal love."[21]

While all traditional religions faced the weakening of their plausibility structures in the nineteenth century through the process of secularization, the contraction of the religious sphere, the experience was often particularly shattering for Jewish intellectuals. As Jacob Talmon has pointed out, "No other group underwent a more thorough break with their former mode of existence than Jews. . . . Nothing existing could any longer be taken for granted."[22] Whereas the secularization of sectors of European society created space for Jews, even secular European culture made use of Christian concepts, symbols, and attitudes that were ostensibly devoid of specific religious meaning. Jews therefore had to confront not only the secularization of their own religious tradition, but their simultaneous entrance into what had been and remained for them a foreign society, contemptuous of most aspects of their culture. Thus, like twentieth century inhabitants of colonialized territories, they were intellectually and ideologically dislocated; their very identity was subject to doubt. As the Jewish historian and radical maskil Isaak Markus Jost wrote in 1833, "All of us who were still children thirty years ago can testify to the incredible changes that have occurred both within and outside us. We have traversed, or better still, flown through a thousand-year history."[23]

This passage from traditional Jewish society to European culture stimulated radicalism among many intellectual Jews. In losing their faith and moorings within the Jewish community, they could not simply adopt European culture wholeheartedly, for it was tinged with Christian doctrines and presuppositions. As Uriel Tal has shown, even German liberals assumed that society, if not the state, must be informed and governed by Christian principles.[24] Because of their historical experience Jewish intellectuals emerged among the foremost promoters of a secular and pluralist society offering equality of opportunity to all, regardless of their origins. They would remake society in the image of their own universalist ideals, to ensure their own belonging and to escape their particularity as Jews. As marginal men, estranged from one society and not yet fully of another, they saw European politics and culture from their own fresh perspective and offered trenchant criticism of societies still so reluctant to accept them fully. Often, they thought, they had little to lose, and much to gain, from the triumph of revolution. Was it not through the French Revolution that Jewish emancipation had first been proclaimed upon European soil? Having experienced radical change and marginality in an especially intense manner, Jewish intellectuals became adept at expressing the traumas of dislocation in a form which resonated among other literate groups. Hence the popularity of Jewish writers from Heinrich Heine to Franz Kafka, who articulated the malaise of living in modern societies. Despite the fact that the majority of Jews were by no means radical in either thought or action, the reality of the Jew who transformed his own experience of marginality and discrimination into a revolutionary stance was sufficient to reinforce the image of Jews as dangerously modern in their politics and culture.

The very mode of Jewish emancipation also linked the Jews to modernity. In every European country liberal political forces were responsible for the conferring of equal rights upon Jews. Politically astute as they were, Jews realized that their fate as citizens depended on the triumph of liberal conceptions of the nation-state and society. Should the Right, with its hierarchic, authoritarian vision of society and its notion of the Christian state, emerge victorious, Jews recognized full well that their civic rights would be rescinded. For this reason they passionately supported liberal parties, even when the latter became ambivalent about "the Jewish question." In the era when liberalism waned, at the close of the last century, Jews achieved the dubious distinction of being the last liberals left in Europe. As the political force responsible for both the French Revolution and the Revolution of 1848, as the political expression of capitalism, liberalism was closely connected with the modern currents within Western societies. And, for obvious reasons, liberalism was also associated in the popular mind with the unfettering of Jews to prey upon the Gentile populace. Thus, in political as well as cultural terms, Jews appeared distinctively modern.

In retrospect, the association of Jews with modernity and its political and cultural attributes has been, at best, a mixed blessing. Liberalism ensured the entry of Jews into the polities and the cultural institutions of the Western world. But its failure, and the backlash it spawned, exposed Jews as the major targets and victims of antimodernist sentiment. Moreover, Jewish survival in the Western world was made more difficult by the unwillingness of European liberals to accept the legitimacy of Jewish assertions of a measure of separatism on a cultural as well as a strictly religious basis. The liberals' denigration of Jewish culture also fostered a pernicious inferiority complex among several generations of modern Jews.

The identification of Jews with the problems generated by modernity is now, I think, largely a relic of the past. While images of Jewish predominance in such areas as the media and finance are notoriously persistent in the popular imagination, those images have become less usable and potent as Jews have become somewhat less distinctive in their socioeconomic profile and as the dire consequences of anti-Semitism have become better appreciated. With the diffusion of modernization throughout much of society, the Jews are no longer so unusually modern.

However, we are still living with the dilemmas of Jewish modernity. On the one hand, many of the values we hold dearest—such as pluralism, democracy, and respect for human rights—have entered our consciousness through our absorption of liberal doctrine. Both in the Diaspora and in Israel we live in two cultures, molded by an inextricable blending of Western and traditional Jewish values, and we are reluctant to give up either. On the other hand, we seek to preserve within the perimeters of an all-consuming, leveling, Western technological culture the particularism of the Jewish tradition and experience. Eager to live in the modern Western world, we yet hope to be able to develop an authentically Jewish critique of the excesses and failures of Western modernity. And we hope likewise to maintain the unity of the Jewish people despite the divergence of the balance of Jewish and Western values in the societies of Israel and the Diaspora and despite the differences in the nature of Jewish identity in Israel, still primarily national, and in the Diaspora, still primarily religious.

One major Jewish problem of the past two centuries has been how to be both Jewish and modern. Many aspects of the problem have been resolved: we no longer struggle for equal rights or wallow in the inferiority complex provoked by entry into Western culture. But the very nature of Jewish identity, of Jewish unity, and of our definition of galut remains problematic. How we answer those questions in the last quarter of our century will determine the state of world Jewry in the postmodern age.

NOTES

1. Cited in Fritz Stern, *The Politics of Cultural Despair* (Garden City, N.Y., 1965), p. 91.

2. Henri Grégoire, *Essai sur la régénération physique, morale, et politique des Juifs* (Metz, 1789), p. 31.

3. Cited in Todd Endelman, *The Jews of Georgian England, 1714–1830: Tradition and Change in a Liberal Society* (Philadelphia, 1979), p. 182.

4. For a fine discussion of the periodization of modern Jewish history, see Michael A. Meyer, "When Does the Modern Period of Jewish History Begin?" *Judaism* 24, no. 3 (Summer 1975): 329–38.

5. Jacob Katz, *Out of the Ghetto* (Cambridge, Mass., 1973), pp. 42–56. This evaluation of Enlightenment society is more pessimistic than the one that Katz elaborated in *Tradition and Crisis* (New York, 1961), in which he labeled the new social circles "the neutral society."

6. See, in particular, Azriel Shohet, *Im Hilufei Tekufot* (Jerusalem, 1960), pp. 58, 131, 162–64. On the Court Jews, see Selma Stern, *The Court Jew* (Philadelphia, 1950), passim; and Hannah Arendt, "Privileged Jews," in *Emancipation and Counter-Emancipation,* ed. Abraham Duker and Meir Ben-Horin (New York, 1974), pp. 60–67.

7. See Endelman, *Jews of Georgian England,* pp. 192–226. On Jewish criminality in Central Europe, see Rudolf Glanz, *Geschichte des niederen jüdischen Volkes in Deutschland* (New York, 1968).

8. Cited in Selma Stern-Tauebler, "The First Generation of Emancipated Jews," *Leo Baeck Institute Yearbook* 16 (1971): 8.

9. For French Jewry, see Phyllis Cohen Albert, *The Modernization of French Jewry: Consistory and Community in the Nineteenth Century* (Hanover, 1977), pp. 26–34. On German Jewry, see Jacob Toury, "Der Eintritt der Juden ins deutsche Bürgertum," in *Das Judentum in der deutschen Umwelt, 1800–1850,* ed. Hans Liebeschutz and Arnold Paucker (Tübingen, 1977), pp. 139–242; and Monika Richarz, *Juedisches Leben in Deutschland, 1780–1871* (New York, 1976), pp. 19–69.

10. Migration patterns can be traced in the civil marriage records, which note the place of birth of the bride and the groom, their current residence, and the domicile of their parents. For the marriage records, see Archives départementales du Bas-Rhin, 4E 330, 4E 226, 5M1 1663. As my study of these records as well as manuscript censuses reveals, fully 20 percent of Alsatian Jews migrated within the region in the first half of the nineteenth century, while other Alsatian Jews moved to Paris or migrated overseas. Alsatian notarial records of the 1850s and 1860s also indicate that 47 percent of the adult children of the deceased lived in locales different from the place of residence of their parents. There is no reason to believe that Alsatian Jews were any more mobile than other Jews throughout Western and Central Europe.

11. A copy of the draft-exemption prayer can be found in the Archives of the Leo Baeck Institute, New York City, West European collection, AR–C 3–19. For an assessment of the rapidity of Jewish modernization, see Steven M. Lowenstein, "The Pace of Modernisation of German Jewry in the Nineteenth Century," *Leo Baeck Institute Yearbook* 21 (1976): 41–56; and Jacob Toury, "'Deutsche Juden' im Vormärz," *Bulletin des Leo Baeck Instituts* 8, no. 29 (1965): 65–82.

12. Paula Hyman, "Jewish Social Mobility in Nineteenth Century Europe: The Case of Alsace," unpublished paper.

13. Ferdinand Tönnies, *Community and Society,* trans. and ed. Charles P. Loomis (New York, 1963), p. 165.

14. Cited in Harvey Goldberg, "Jean Jaurès and the Jewish Question: The Evolution of a Position," *Jewish Social Studies* 20, no. 2 (April 1958): 1.

15. Cited in Theodore S. Hamerow, "The German Artisan Movement, 1848–49," *Journal of Central European Affairs* 21, no. 2 (July 1961), pp. 135–52.

16. For the latest account of antimodernism, see Shulamith Volkov, *The Rise of Popular Anti-Modernism in Germany* (Princeton, 1978).

17. Cited in George Mosse, *The Crisis of German Ideology* (New York, 1964), p. 23.

18. Peter Gay, *Freud, Jews, and Other Germans* (London and New York, 1978), pp. 93–108.

19. Romain Rolland, *Jean Christophe,* trans. Gilbert Cannan (New York, 1910–13), book 2, p. 384.

20. Peter Berger, *The Sacred Canopy* (Garden City, N.Y., 1967), pp. 127–35.

21. Berr Isaac Berr, *Lettre d'un citoyen* (Nancy, 1791), p. 16.

22. Jacob Talmon, "Jews between Revolution and Counter-Revolution," in *Israel among the Nations* (London, 1970), pp. 17–18. For the most useful survey of Jewish revolutionaries, see Robert Wistrich, *Revolutionary Jews from Marx to Trotsky* (New York, 1976).

23. Cited in Ismar Schorsch, "From Wolfenbuettel to Wissenschaft: The Divergent Paths of Isaak Markus Jost and Leopold Zunz," *Leo Baeck Institute Yearbook* 22 (1977): 110.

24. Uriel Tal, *Christians and Jews in Germany,* trans. Noah Jonathan Jacobs (Ithaca, N.Y.: 1975), pp. 160–76.

American Jews and the Swiss Treaty: A Case Study in the Indivisibility of Anti-Semitism

Naomi W. Cohen

Hunter College, City University of New York

Emancipation of the Jews in the nineteenth and twentieth centuries dramatically changed the lives of individual Jews and the course of Jewish history. In countries which granted Jews citizenship on an equal basis with others, the Jewish community—heretofore a legally chartered entity with a substantial amount of autonomy—was officially disbanded. The modern national state had no room for a corporate group with separate schools, courts, and civil law. The Jew in the eyes of the law was absorbed into the body politic as an individual. His nationality— French, English, American—came first. His ties to the Jewish group were secondary, peripheral, and voluntary. Many predicted that those ties would eventually be eroded completely.

But the promulgation of new laws and even the razing of ghetto walls could not automatically change Christian thinking about Jews. Emancipation never entirely dispelled the premodern image of a Jewish collective body that was somehow larger than the sum of its parts. To the Christian, more than sectarian differences separated, and continued to separate, the Jew from his compatriots. The old stereotypes of the Jew as eternal alien, Christ killer, Shylock, and plotter against Christians and Christendom still flourished, even in places where there were no Jews. Those images enveloped all Jews, irrespective of nationality. Thus, the modern Jew soon learned that no matter what the law, Christian fear and hatred linked him with Jews all over the world. He came to see that even in the modern world anti-Semitism was indivisible and very likely to cross national boundaries. Discrimination against Jews in any corner of the world ultimately involved him.

It was difficult for nineteenth century American Jews in particular to admit that they shared a vulnerability with Jews abroad. They had settled in a New World, which since the eighteenth century had been hailed by non-Jewish ideologues as the promised land. Jews wanted to believe that their history had turned a corner when it reached the United States, that just as America had broken away from a decadent Old World to establish the ideal free society, so would America be the noble experiment in the Jewish experience. The nineteenth century Jewish leaders often pointed to the status they enjoyed and to marks of favor bestowed by their government upon individual Jews (e.g., appointments to official posts) as lessons on how Jews should be treated that America was teaching the rest of the world.

In theory at least, it might have appeared that Jews in the United States would inevitably slough off their sense of a common destiny with other Jews. After all, many of their foreign brethren were still unemancipated, but they, because of their country's exceptionalism, enjoyed a seeming immunity to the torments and tortures so familiar in the Jewish past.

Two factors, however, qualified their optimism and their sense of distinctiveness. First, America itself was not free of the mythic stereotypes or various manifestations of anti-Semitism. Indeed, it could not have been otherwise in a land to which immigrants brought with them Old World ideas and prejudices. When anti-Semitism reared its head in America, or when European anti-Semites lumped American Jews along with all the others, Jews slowly learned that their American nationality made little difference.

More important, American Jews, like Jews throughout the world, were the bearers and guardians of a corporate memory, a sense of peoplehood, which they were not ready to relinquish. Linked by a common heritage with Jews elsewhere, they were steeped in a religious tradition which imposed the responsibility of one for all. They conscientiously shouldered burdens of relief for their less fortunate foreign brethren, tasks which joined freethinker with synagogue member, Orthodox Jew with Reform Jew. But more subtle than the responses of philanthropy and defense was an emotional empathy generated by the Jewish heritage. "It is manifestly ordained by the Supreme Ruler of the Universe," Boston's Jews said on one occasion in the mid-1850s, "that the children of Israel, however widely dispersed, living under different governments, in different climes, and speaking different languages, should still feel united in sympathy and sentiment; that the woes, joys and triumphs of one or a few of them, find a 'ready response' in the bosoms of the whole race."[1]

The faith in America's exceptionalism never really quashed the belief in a common Jewish destiny and the attendant acceptance of the indivisibility of anti-Semitism. Yet, what was to become patently clear to the American Jewish community after the Nazi era was less apparent to their nineteenth century forebears. The Jews first needed to translate the *religious* doctrine of group responsibility into modern *secular* and political terms.

American Jewish responses to the Damascus affair and to the discriminatory American-Swiss treaty, which are treated in the following discussion, were the first signs of awareness that equality under American law did not guarantee American Jews a unique kind of immunity. Only then did they begin to learn some basic facts of Jewish life: (1) that to combat anti-Semitism abroad was a matter of self-interest and not mere philanthropy, (2) that foreign governments which recognized the rights of Jews of one country would be hard put to discriminate against those of another, and (3) that a nation which did not protest anti-Jewish discrimination in another land was in effect condoning that discrimination and implicitly threatening thereby the security of its own Jews.

84

Before the Civil War it appeared reasonable for American Jews to assume that if enlightened countries discriminated against Jews, progress could not be expected in less liberal nations. Thus, for example, the Board of Delegates of American Israelites, the first American Jewish defense agency, pointed out in 1860 that North Carolina's refusal to permit Jews to hold office held up the relaxation of restrictions on Jews in other countries. Freedom too, American Jews believed, was contagious. In 1858, when Jews were finally permitted to take seats in Parliament, one Baltimore Jew commented that England's action would dispose its European neighbors more favorably toward Jews "than all the deputations that could be sent to them."[2]

Despite the conviction that freedom and its absence spun indivisible webs, most American Jews still stopped short of linking their own security directly with that of the victims of European anti-Semitism. At the same time, they resolutely affirmed their loyalty to their foreign brethren on two levels. First, it was incumbent upon the Jews in free countries to display exemplary conduct—to prove, as it were, that freedom for the Jew was a safe investment for all nations.[3] Second, just because they enjoyed a more fortunate position, their responsibility for ameliorating the plight of the less advantaged was, if anything, increased.

Fortunately for American Jews, the United States, a nation of immigrants, saw nothing wrong with this concern for fellow Jews in foreign lands. Other minorities too engaged in relief drives and in various forms of agitation for securing the freedom of coreligionists or coethnics. On occasion some might grumble that Jews were sending too much money in the form of relief out of the country,[4] but for the most part Christians commended the fervor with which Jews responded to their less fortunate brethren.

Moreover, the interest of American Jews in the conditions of foreign Jews dovetailed with the concept of the American mission. During the Revolution, Benjamin Franklin had summed up America's belief in its appointed role to serve as the exemplar of liberty for the entire world: "Establishing the liberties of America will not only make that people happy, but will have some effect in diminishing the misery of those, who in other parts of the world groan under despotism. . . . our cause is esteemed the cause of all mankind. . . . We are fighting for the dignity and happiness of all mankind."[5] Against that canvas, Americans who called upon Old World governments to desist from tyranny and to recognize human rights were only acting out the national creed. The belief in the American mission accounted for the optimistic hope in the first half of the nineteenth century that revolutionary struggles in other lands—the Spanish-American colonies, Greece, Hungary—were being waged in emulation of the American example. American Jewry found encouragement in the outpouring of American sympathy for those revolutionary movements and for the rebels who suffered at the hands of despotic regimes. True, the government avoided direct intervention in the conflicts, but the idea persisted that the United States had the right, if not the responsibility, to engage in humanitarian diplomacy, to speak out on behalf of political freedom and in defense of human rights.[6]

The American reaction to the Damascus blood libel of 1840 offers a classic textbook case of humanitarian diplomacy. The libel arose when a priest in Damascus and his servant suddenly disappeared. The Ottoman government, suspicious that the Jews might have killed the two Catholics, immediately entered the Jewish quarter and tortured several Jews until confessions to murder were elicited. The Jews supposedly admitted that the blood of the missing pair had been drained for use in baking matzot for Passover and that the bodies had then been hacked into small pieces. The Ottoman government stepped up its tortures, determined to find the bottles of Catholic blood. At first report, seventy-two Jews were sentenced to be hanged, but the entire Damascus Jewish community, comprising perhaps as many as 30,000 Jews, was under suspicion.[7]

Upon hearing of the British protests against the persecution of the Damascus Jews, John Forsyth, the American secretary of state, informed the American representatives in Egypt and Turkey of America's horror over the revival of the barbaric blood libel charge and of its sympathy with the Jewish victims. Forsyth wrote that President Van Buren desired the repression of "these horrors," and he justified America's intervention in the affair.

> The President is of the opinion, that from no one can such generous endeavors proceed with so much propriety and effect, as from the Representative of a friendly power, whose institutions, political and civil, place upon the same footing, the worshippers of God, of every faith and form, acknowledging no distinction between the Mahomedan, the Jews, and the Christian. Should you in carrying out these instructions find it necessary or proper to address yourself to any of the Turkish authorities you will refer to this distinctive character-istic of our government, as investing with a peculiar propriety and right the interposition of your good offices in behalf of an oppressed and persecuted race among whose kindred are found some of the most worthy and patriotic of our citizens.[8]

The government's reaction cannot be dismissed as a political favor to the 15,000 Americans Jews; the executive responded *before* the Jews petitioned for interces-sion. Forsyth's formulation, that it was America's place, in light of its democratic structure, to intercede, also illustrates how humanitarian diplomacy derived from the mission concept.

American Jews learned of the Damascus affair from Jews abroad. At several mass meetings which took place weeks after the administration had acted, Jews also cited America's mission as reason for official protest. Since they saw the blood libel as a blow against enlightenment and civilization, and thus a threat to humanity at large, they insisted that it rightfully deserved the condemnation of Jew and Christian alike. Buoyed up by a sympathetic public and by the government's response, the Jews of Richmond confidently interpreted Van Buren's action as a hopeful sign for the future. His "voluntary act," they said, "assures to us his sympathy in whatever may hereafter be attempted or done toward extending to the ancient race of Israel, wherever dispersed, the civil and religious privileges secured to us by the Constitution of this favored land."[9]

For Americans, the Damascus affair turned out to be one of those rare occasions on which all participants won. The government, free of conflicting pressures or interests in the Middle East, advanced its image as a protector of universal freedom. Concerned Christians could reap satisfaction insofar as the public outcry from the free world halted the persecution in Syria.[10] The American Jews too emerged victorious. Their faith in the beneficence of their government and in the efficacy of rational appeals to public opinion was vindicated. They found reason for pride and gratification in the expression of Christian sympathy, for it meant that in the eyes of their compatriots the cause of the Jews was as important as that of other oppressed groups.[11]

The component of American Jewish self-interest in the Damascus affair, albeit low-key, was not totally absent. At a meeting of Philadelphia's Jews, the speakers called the blood libel a "calumny" against Judaism. One of them ventured further: "If such a calumny is not nipped in the bud, its effect will not be limited to any particular place, but will be extended to every part of the globe."[12] Even if most American Jews could not imagine being subjected to torture, the charge that Jews used Christian blood for their Passover rites constituted a blot upon their faith and called for vigorous denials.

Those who feared that the libel's influence could reach American shores were proved correct a decade later. On April 6, 1850, the *New York Herald,* which had originally sympathized with the Jews of Damascus, reopened the charges with a lurid front-page story of how an atrocious murder had been perpetrated by the Jews, acting according to mysterious talmudic injuctions, and of how the investigation of the murder had been squelched by the devious manipulations of the House of Rothschild. The *Herald*'s account was potentially far more dangerous to American Jews than the original episode. As the *Asmonean,* a New York Jewish weekly, pointed out, not only could the story "kindle afresh that latent bigotry which may be smoldering in weak minds," but it linked the "mysteries" of the Jewish religion with the archsymbol of nineteenth century Jewish secular power.[13] It thereby made the Jewish peril this-worldly, immediate, and a potential danger to Western society—and hence more credible to an American audience.

Ten years after the Damascus affair, discrimination by a foreign government again aroused the concern of American Jews. This time, however, the traditional roles were reversed. Switzerland was the oppressor; the United States was a partner in discrimination rather than the detached symbol of universal rights; and American Jews were the immediate victims instead of the rescuers. The matter arose in connection with a treaty of commerce negotiated in 1850 by the United States and Switzerland. In its original form the treaty explicitly stated: "On account of the tenor of the Federal Constitution of Switzerland, Christians alone are entitled to the enjoyment of the privileges guaranteed by the present Article in the Swiss Cantons."[14] Since Switzerland's constitution guaranteed the right of religious freedom only to Christians, and since Switzerland was a federal republic,

87

its cantons had the right, which some put to use, of refusing entry and commercial privileges to foreign Jews. Bound by its constitution, the central government could make no exception for American Jews. To the latter's chagrin, the United States accepted the draft treaty with its discriminatory feature, thus setting the American Jews apart from their fellow citizens.

Although that was the aspect which rankled the most, the problem went deeper. If Switzerland were to admit American Jews, it would first have to let down the barriers against Jews in general. A. Dudley Mann, the American minister who negotiated the treaty, had reported to the State Department that the restrictions were not expressions of religious bigotry but were safeguards employed by the cantons against a feared influx of Alsatian Jews.[15] Most American Jews, however, did not plan to merge their fight with the cause of all Jews. In fact, since Swiss discrimination did not reach dramatic proportions, American Jews ignored it until they became involved personally.

In January 1851 the *Asmonean* opened the first round of protest against the treaty. Both the newspaper and Dr. Sigmund Waterman, a German-born Jewish liberal who took the lead in mobilizing the initial opposition, blamed Mann for the flagrant insult to the Jews. Although Switzerland had the undisputed right to regulate the status of Jews in its own land, the United States could not be a party to those laws. For an American diplomat to accept a treaty that denied equal rights to an important segment of the American people was unconscionable.[16]

Mann was well aware of the discriminatory clause, but he took refuge in the reasoning that since the treaty did not *compel* the cantons to exclude Jews, individual Jews from America who desired to live and trade in Switzerland would probably not be turned away. He later claimed that he had gone along with the discrimination only reluctantly, warning the Swiss that the president or the Senate might well hold up ratification on that account.[17]

Since the treaty had not yet reached the Senate, the *Asmonean* called on Jews to agitate against its passage. It also urged Christians to add their protest. A matter of principle was at stake; besides, if discrimination against one group were tolerated, it could be turned against other groups. Roused by the newspaper, a number of New York Jews drew up a memorial to the Senate, and individuals in other cities also communicated their opposition to Secretary of State Daniel Webster. Webster, President Fillmore, and Senator Clay agreed with the petitioners. A number of senators approached by the *Asmonean* and the *Occident,* Rabbi Isaac Leeser's prestigious Anglo-Jewish monthly, also sided with the Jewish position.

Most of the protests from the Jews defined the issue in terms of religious intolerance and claimed that the United States government could not discriminate among its citizens or deny rights to Jews on religious grounds. Worried lest the United States acknowledge Christianity to be the dominant religion, the Jewish protesters also recounted the virtues and patriotism of the country's Jews. Dr. Waterman invoked "higher law" in defense of the Jewish case. He argued that international treaties were supposed to overcome rather than foster bigotry. In addition, since Americans had entrusted their well-being to a representative government which was bound by a social contract to protect their rights, that government could not disable a portion of its citizens or barter away the rights of any of the parties to religious freedom.[18]

It should be pointed out that, technically, religious freedom was not at stake. Acceptance of the treaty by the United States in no way deprived American Jews, even those few who might want to establish themselves in Switzerland, of the right to worship as they pleased. More accurately, the issue was one of equality of religion: American Jews were agitating *against* their government's acquiescence in discrimination rather than *for* equal rights in Switzerland. The important objective was to get the American, and not the Swiss, government to admit that Jews were equal to Christians in the eye of the law and to refrain from enacting any invidious distinctions.

In 1851, American Jews were actuated principally by self-interest. Nevertheless, they had to consider two other aspects of the treaty issue: the effect of the treaty on the American image and the impact that the treaty would have on other governments which oppressed the Jews. The *Asmonean* editorialized on America's worldwide influence, on how Europe looked to the United States for guidance. Since America was historically the refuge for persons seeking religious freedom, it was morally obligated to reject the discriminatory treaty. Hadn't Secretary Daniel Webster informed the Austrian representative in 1850 that the United States could not help but sympathize with political struggles against absolutism? Senator Henry Clay agreed in a letter to Dr. Waterman: "This is not the country nor the age in which ancient and unjust prejudices should receive any countenance."

Ironically, it seems that the *Asmonean* was reminded of America's responsibilities by Jews in Switzerland. It published a letter from some Swiss Jews of the Argau canton which begged the Americans to work against the treaty's passage. The Swiss put the issue in dramatic terms: "Should the narrow-mindedness of a European Republic succeed in thus polluting that holy ground, where the ashes of Washington and Franklin rest?"[19]

Although the *Asmonean* never claimed that its fight against the treaty was also a struggle against Swiss prejudice, it no doubt remembered the interdependence of Jewish freedom in different countries. When the Senate ultimately rejected the objectionable clause, the paper happily concluded that Switzerland and its neighbors, particularly the German states, which were still rife with oppression, had been taught a significant lesson.[20]

Once aroused, American Jewish interest in the Swiss situation persisted after the treaty as amended by the Senate had been returned to Berne. In 1852, articles in the *Asmonean* and the *Occident* called attention to Swiss repression of the Jews in general and to France's activities on behalf of its Jewish nationals. Isaac Mayer

Wise, then a rabbi in Albany, urged that a conference of congregational representatives be held in New York to formulate a petition asking that the government protest the "inhuman and degrading" Swiss policies. The leading propagator of Reform Judaism, a movement which labored arduously to discard the ethnic component of Judaism, now said that it was the "sacred duty" of American Jews to let their brethren in Switzerland know "that our hearts bleed because of their misery; that we weep when we remember Zion." Wise confidently predicted that the American government would heed the petition and that its "powerful word . . . will check the enemies of Israel." Congregation Anshe Emeth in Albany accordingly registered its protest against Switzerland and selected a delegate for the proposed conference. In New York City, Shaar Hashamaim followed suit. Resolutions by that congregation went farther, tying the interests of the Swiss Jews to those of the American Jews. Even if the petition to the United States government failed to bring about emancipation in Switzerland, they said, "still we deem the movement one of momentous interest to our people in general, in asmuch [sic] as it will show tyranical [sic] and unjust powers that the Jew, a citizen of this country, is entitled to, and must enjoy, as much liberty in these countries, as the most favored citizen of this great Republic, if accident, business, or pleasure should draw his steps thither."[21]

The conference that Wise urged never materialized, but the very suggestion proved that the idea of fighting the prejudice directed against Jews elsewhere, as opposed merely to countering the fallout of that prejudice on American Jews, had vaguely penetrated the Jewish community. It also brought the Jews closer to those Americans who were then pressing for the rights of American Protestants in Catholic countries. In 1854, when a Senate committee recommended that in future treaties the United States seek to secure the right to worship for its citizens (citizens, and not merely Christians), Senator Lewis Cass, who steered the resolution to its passage, invited the Jews to add their petitions on the matter. Captain Jonas P. Levy, a prominent Washingtonian, organized the response, and a Jewish memorial, insisting that foreign countries reciprocate the privileges that the United States afforded their citizens, was forwarded to the Senate. Although the Jewish memorial did not point up peculiarly Jewish needs, in presenting it to the Senate, Cass did. The senator said in part:

> Exposed as the members of this persuasion yet are in portions of Europe and America, both Protestant and Catholic, to the most illiberal prejudices and to religious disabilities, the position of our citizens abroad who belong to it has peculiar claims to the consideration and interposition of the government. Beside their legal right to equal protection there is no portion of our population whose peaceable and law-abiding conduct better proves than theirs does, that they are well entitled to all the privileges secured to every American by our system of government.

Sympathetic but patronizing, Cass did not mention Switzerland, but the situation in Switzerland doubtless colored the thinking of the Jews, for the revised Swiss treaty was then under consideration by the Senate.[22]

Favorable action on the resolution defending the religious rights of Americans abroad did not inhibit the Senate from approving the second draft of the Swiss treaty. Formally ratified in 1855, the treaty contained no references to exclusively Christian rights, but it did provide that the rights of domicile and commerce obtained only if they were not in conflict with cantonal law. The inequity which still left American Jews at the mercy of the individual cantons had been noted by Wise's *Israelite* and Leeser's *Occident.* When Leeser brought it to Cass's attention, the latter made reassuring sounds but really skirted the issue. A few secular newspapers also commented on the amended treaty's violation of equal rights, but apparently the eventual passage of the new draft went unnoticed by most Jews.[23]

Interest was sparked anew when Jews learned that a Mr. A. H. Gootman, an American Jewish merchant, had been ordered to leave the canton of Neuchâtel just because he was a Jew. Although the American minister to Switzerland succeeded in obtaining an exemption for Gootman, the principle that cantons could exclude Jews at will remained unchanged.[24] The Gootman case evoked a new round of agitation within the Jewish community.[25] In 1857, at protest meetings in various cities, the Swiss treaty was denounced by Jews, sometimes joined by Christians. The meetings drew up petitions to the government and formulated plans to send delegations to President Buchanan. The Jewish periodicals worked actively to generate and sustain an effective opposition, encouraging their readers neither to cringe nor to indulge in "impotent rage." The *Asmonean* boldly counseled that the Jews be uninhibited about using their numbers, wealth, and commercial position to proper advantage.

The chorus of indignation exceeded that of 1851, but the principal argument remained the same. From the Midwest, the South, and the Atlantic seaboard the Jewish cry for equality reverberated. The discriminatory treaty, according to its critics, violated the spirit, if not the letter, of the Constitution, and it merited the opposition of all Americans. Some argued that by permitting Switzerland to screen American citizens the federal government was acceding to a test oath, which was expressly forbidden by the Constitution. Others charged that the treaty was unconstitutional because it violated the general welfare clause! It was suggested that those who actually experienced discrimination at the hands of the Swiss sue the American government for damages and test the treaty's constitutionality before the Supreme Court.[26]

Understandably, the Jews were more bitter in 1857 than they had been in 1851. Despite assurances to the contrary by Senator Cass, who was now secretary of state, discrimination had somehow been "smuggled in." The Senate could not be excused; we were sold out, some lamented, perhaps, as Rabbi Isaac Leeser explained, because the government did not think us important enough. The non-Jewish press repeated the conspiracy charge, and the administration's political foes had a field day attacking the Democrats.

Most Jews refrained from making the issue a partisan one. The Jews of Easton, Pennsylvania, were an exception; calling themselves good Democrats, they lashed out against their party. Timidity and the habitual reluctance of nineteenth century Western Jews to inject themselves qua Jews into politics acted as restraining influences. The Jews preferred to describe the issue as American and nonsectarian, and they bemoaned America's betrayal of its international image. They, a group of loyal and law-abiding citizens rooted in their "second Canaan," were being deprived of rights under a treaty which brought only little benefit to the United States. Their logic demanded that the treaty be abrogated, or at least that its objectionable clause be nullified.

Jewish leaders were also quick to fault their coreligionists for helping to bring about a deplorable situation. Had the Jews been attentive to the diplomatic negotiations in 1854, had the community been united or prepared to take concerted action, the damage might have been averted. The traditionalist *Occident* injected its running feud with the Reform Jews into the matter by insinuating that the community had been lulled into a false security by the "reform doctors." While the latter behaved as if the redemption of the Jews had arrived, the rights of Jews, even in America, were still in danger. "We are in *Galuth*," Leeser wrote; "we have our theoretical rights; but practically they are dependent on the will of those who have numbers on their side; and if we make all the noise in the world, and brag aloud after our heart's content, *we are yet strangers* in stranger lands."[27]

Leeser's baleful editorial reminded American Jews of their ties to Jews all over the world; the fetters that bound one were felt by all. Isaac Mayer Wise, Leeser's archcompetitor in theology and in the publishing field, agreed in his periodical, the *Israelite,* that "Kol Yisrael 'arevim zeh ba-zeh," and he urged cooperation between French and American Jews on the Swiss matter. American Jews recalled how a Swiss rabbi had watched the progress of the treaty, and they coupled their concern over that matter with an interest in the conditions of the Swiss Jews.[28] But although they may have felt united with the Europeans by the same forces of discrimination, they actively sought remediation for themselves only.

In October 1857 a national convention of Jewish delegates on the treaty was held in Baltimore. A breakdown in communication and severe internal bickering prevented the emergence of any body that could really be called representative of American Jewry, but the truncated convention, made up of Jews from only four states, dispatched a delegation to the president. The delegates found Buchanan most gracious. He assured them that had the treaty's inequities been understood properly, his predecessor would not have approved it. The Jews readily accepted that explanation as well as the president's promise to resolve the problem. Wise, who took part in the meeting, then advised that the communal agitation cease.

While the episode smacks of Jewish timidity, its impact was more positive than might have been expected. In the wake of the meeting and of the numerous memorials presented to the executive, the secretary of state informed the American minister to Switzerland that the president was most anxious to have the discriminatory clause removed.[29]

The official in Berne who received Secretary Cass's instructions was Theodore S. Fay. A native of New York, Fay had been trained for the bar but had chosen to pursue literary work instead. In 1836 the twenty-nine-year-old writer, who had already published a best-selling novel, was appointed to his first diplomatic post. An uninterrupted career in diplomacy followed; from the office of secretary at the Berlin legation he was promoted in 1853 to serve as minister to Switzerland. A devout Christian, Fay was admired for his diplomatic skills. The *New York Times,* which in 1857 roundly criticized the ineptitude of Buchanan's diplomatic appointees, singled out Fay as the notable exception.[30]

Fay was well aware of the Jewish grievance long before he received Cass's instructions. He had interceded with the Swiss authorities on behalf of Gootman. Later he learned of the Jewish agitation on the treaty through American newspapers. He thought it well-nigh impossible to do away with the discriminatory clause so long as the existing Swiss constitutional structure remained unchanged. Furthermore, it was clear to him that the admission of American Jews was repugnant to the Swiss primarily because it would mean opening the door to all Jews, even the objectionable Alsatians.

There were other obstacles blocking the path to amelioration. England and France had put forth requests on behalf of their Jews and had been turned down. Moreover, America's case rested not on legal right but solely on comity, and the United States had to tread lightly lest it alienate or embarrass the Swiss federal government. Meanwhile, Switzerland, determined to resist American pressure, made it known through its consul-general in Washington that it would entertain no further correspondence on the matter. Finally, even if the Swiss federal government were more sympathetic, it could always plead incompetence by disclaiming any influence over the cantons.

In spite of the difficulties, Fay promised to do what he could. He admitted that the grievance was just and that the Swiss treaty impinged upon the dignity of free governments like the United States. Nevertheless, he too, at this time, seemingly accepted the popular stereotypes of the usurious and unpalatable Alsatians. Cautioning Washington not to expect too much, Fay undertook to tackle the problem by preparing a careful study of the numbers and the conditions of the Jews in the various cantons. He asked the cantons to supply the information and to add their reasons for denying entry to American Jews. His plan was to air the findings in a public note along with his own rebuttals against discrimination. His efforts, perhaps, would arouse a more liberal public opinion, which in turn would induce the cantons to change their regulations.

As the American minister, Fay carefully limited his official inquiries to the issue of American Jews. But since the real object of discrimination was the Alsatian Jews, and since American Jews were being penalized because of them, he planned a broader project. He would fight for the rights of the American Jews along with the defense of the Alsatian Jews. Unconcerned with the theoretical issue of how far prejudice was indivisible, Fay, for strictly pragmatic purposes, linked the status of the two Jewish groups.

Fay's note, which took a year and a half to prepare, involved the minister in intensive and far-flung research. He supplemented his analysis of the cantonal data with a visit to Alsace in the company of a Swiss rabbi. From a Protestant clergyman he learned how some cantons denied burial rights to Jews under their jurisdiction. Fay also turned to American Jews, asking them (through the State Department) for information on the economic and social position of the Jews in the United States and on the progress made in gaining civil rights for Jews in other countries. The tenor of the inquiry, which drew a woefully inadequate response, indicates that Fay hoped to show Switzerland, first, that its policies regarding Jews were archaic in comparison with the policies of other countries, and second, that the Jews from America who were liable to exclusion were a most desirable element. His implied argument, that one country could not hold back on rights to Jews against the march of progress, lent further substance to the principle of the indivisibility of both freedom and prejudice.

Meanwhile the minister kept the issue alive through diplomatic channels. Two other cases of American Jews being denied the right of residence proved that it was not merely an academic problem. Fay pressed the federal officials to secure the information he wanted from the cantons. He reminded them of President Buchanan's ongoing concern over the matter as well as of the economic advantages which Switzerland derived from the treaty. Defending the right of the United States to study the value of the treaty, he argued against Switzerland's move to terminate the discussion. In a forceful dispatch to the federal council, Fay warned that if the problem could not be aired, he would tell his government that there was no foundation for the restriction on Jews. He spoke warmly on behalf of rights for American Jews, rights which belonged to them as American citizens and were sanctioned by the spirit of international comity, civilized usage, and Christianity. When the Swiss president again invoked the claim of cantonal sovereignty, Fay boldly announced that he was prepared to negotiate separately with the cantonal governments. He also left with the Swiss officials articles from the American Jewish press on the agitation against the treaty, confident that they would be communicated to the cantons.

When it became known in Berne that the American minister was preparing an in-depth study, anti-Jewish discrimination became a popular subject within the diplomatic corps and among the public at large. A Berne newspaper even denounced one canton for its illiberal restrictions. Since that paper reflected the views of the Swiss vice-president, and since it had earlier attacked the constitution for its limits on free religious worship, Fay concluded that a dent had been made in public opinion. Fay himself became more sympathetic to the plight of the Jews as his research progressed. Convinced now that the charges against the Alsatians amounted only to unfounded prejudice, he believed that his note would effectively silence them.[31]

In May 1859 Fay presented his lengthy note to the Swiss government.[32] After a detailed review of the policies of the different cantons toward Jews, he summarized the effect of the restrictive laws on the American Jews. Suggesting that economic jealousy was an important obstacle to the acceptance of Jews as equals, the minister protested the humiliations that had been heaped upon his countrymen, particularly since the American Jews had suffered worse treatment than the Swiss Jews or the Jews of other countries.

Fay enumerated and countered all the reasons that had been advanced to uphold the restrictions. When he considered the argument that Christianity justified anti-Jewish discrimination, he transcended his role as American diplomat and defended the rights of all Jews in the modern world. Speaking as a devout believer and, incidentally, as one who accepted the superiority of Christianity over Judaism, Fay wrote:

> Of all the errors of the last eighteen centuries there is not a greater than the supposition that every wrong or insult to the Hebrew nation is commanded or justified by the Bible. The exact contrary is the case. The treatment which this people have received since the destruction of their city was, it is true, predicted both by the Old and New Testaments, as various other events. But so were earthquakes, and wars, and other calamities and crimes. . . . It is stated that, not only they are to be regarded by Christians as the chosen people of God, and to be restored to their country, and to a preeminence among other nations, but that all the wrongs inflicted upon them by the governments and peoples of the world will be regarded as sins and so punished. . . . Hence, throughout all christendom [*sic*], the present century has seen a gradually extended movement in favor of the Israelites; and statesmen and legislatures who support, and populations which demand, constitutional clauses excluding them, in the supposition that such clauses are required or even sanctioned by the volume believed in by Christians, consult neither the letter nor the spirit nor the true interests of Christianity, but rather the exclusiveness of ancient Judaism. All the reasons for persecuting Jews are equally unjust and wrong, and while political economists explode the idea that their presence injures a nation, and the Christian has discovered that their persecution is displeasing to God, the student of history is amazed at the calumnies of which they have been the victims, and can no more admit that their emancipation would be prejudicial to a country than that Judaism can overthrow or endanger Christianity, or that the Israelites ever poisoned the public wells and fountains, or used the blood of Christian infants at their feast of the passover.[33]

Another reason given to condone the restrictions, the fear of Alsatian Jews, was in Fay's opinion the principal one. The minister disputed the popular notion that a Switzerland totally free of restrictions would be inundated by neighboring Jewish peddlers and swindlers, and he cited facts and figures proving that Alsatian Jews were moving increasingly into "respectable" occupations. Experience in modern countries, Fay asserted, proved that "the better the Israelites are treated the more that class of them which has caused annoyance to Switzerland improves. Restrictive and proscriptive legislations have a tendency to create and to maintain the demoralization, and the ignorant Israelite becomes a usurer only when other legitimate paths of profit are closed against him."[34]

Having shifted his comments to Jews in general, Fay continued:

It is certain, at the present day, that the moral character of the great majority of persons calling themselves Christians would not justify the exclusion of the Hebrew people from any country existing. Why should not a respectable Israelite hold land as well as a respectable Christian? Why should an immoral Israelite hold land as well as an immoral Christian? Any why should thousands of moral and honest Israelites be excluded, when domicile is accorded to any and every immoral person merely calling himself a Christian? Baron Rothschild cannot purchase a foot in the restrictive cantons, yet any atheist may buy what he likes; and persons under the name of Christians, but who openly mock at all religion, may come in crowds, and trade, and sell, and buy, and worship where they like, or not worship at all. True, every Israelite is not like Baron Rothschild, but neither is every Christian. Neither is every Jew a swindler or a usurer.

Fay then dwelt on the fact that in Western Europe and the United States Jews were to be found in high political and social positions. He said:

In proportion as they have been relieved from persecution, they have, without injurious consequences, mingled more freely and equally in the affairs of society; the highest professions and fields of art have received lustre from their genius, and the undersigned can testify, from experience as well as observation, that in the common walks of life they furnish examples of fidelity and honesty, as well as intelligence and zeal, which might redress the alarm of thousands calling themselves Christians.[35]

From Fay's point of view, his efforts brought about positive results. His note was translated into French and German and widely circulated; copies were even sold by the Swiss federal council. Swiss newspapers reported on it favorably, and public opinion seemed to support an end to restrictions. The French and British ministers promised to cooperate in prodding the Swiss, and the Bavarian minister told Fay that if the United States won its point, the Bavarian Jews would gain their emancipation.[36]

American Jews were less sanguine. They had not been informed of Fay's strategy, and although they welcomed the appearance of the note they did not see any immediate or tangible gains. True, their agitation, which had originally set into motion the process culminating in the note, may have contributed to the finished product. In accord with their position, Fay wrote in forceful terms that American Jews abroad had the right to demand equal protection from their government. Nevertheless, the most irksome issue had not changed—the United States was still a party to anti-Jewish discrimination. To the further dismay of American Jews, the United States government entered into a treaty with China in 1860 which, while establishing the right of all American citizens to residential and commercial privileges, specifically provided for the protection of the Christian religion. The newly organized Board of Delegates of American Israelites noted almost wistfully in its first report that equal protection for Jews had, "up to this time, been very feebly recognized by the treaty-making power."[37]

Jews did not cease their agitation entirely. The Board of Delegates, taking up the function of the ad hoc committees of 1857, appealed to the State Department, and it joined forces with European Jewish groups which were pressing for the removal of the Swiss disabilities. In 1866 the Board announced that the restrictions had been lifted.[38] However, the victory was only partial, for the United States, by failing to denounce the treaty, had never admitted the rectitude of the Jewish plea for equality. That humiliation continued to rankle. In 1903 a young Jewish lawyer who wrote the first historical account of the Swiss affair injected the following sentence into an otherwise dry and emotionless narrative: "It was demonstrated to us that while we were American citizens, our citizenship was distinctly qualified— we were and we are American-Jewish citizens, at least as far as our international rights were and are concerned."[39]

Had the American Jews not concentrated almost exclusively on the demand for equal treatment from their government, they, like Fay, would have consciously worked out the principle of the indivisibility of prejudice. As has been pointed out, they acknowledged that principle in theory, and some ideas raised between 1851 and 1860 show that, at least tacitly, they admitted that the acceptance of American Jews was contingent upon the acceptance of all Jews.

Fifty years later, in the case of Russian discrimination against American Jews, a new generation of communal leaders built a campaign on that very principle. In the Russian episode the issue was again one of American Jewish equality. Despite a treaty of 1832 which guaranteed reciprocal rights to Russians and Americans in each other's countries, the tsarist government imposed economic and residential restrictions on American Jews. Since the United States passively accepted Russia's actions, American Jews were stigmatized as second-class citizens. Accordingly, under the leadership of the American Jewish Committee they successfully carried through a fight for the abrogation of the treaty.

Lasting from 1908 through 1911, the campaign against the treaty drew from the earlier techniques of Jewish agitation. Albeit in a more planned and refined fashion, it too made use of public protest meetings and resolutions, Christian allies, visits to the president and other public figures, and contacts with foreign Jewish groups. Most important, however, the activists knowingly or unknowingly took a leaf from Fay's book. Although they highlighted the discrimination against American Jews, their primary objective was to compel Russia to emancipate its own Jews. They reasoned that if the Russian government, under the threat of abrogation, granted rights to American Jews, it could not do less for the Jews of Russia. Thus, just as Fay had fought for Alsatians in order to get rights for Americans, the American Jewish Committee fought for Americans in order to get rights for the Russians.[40]

The campaign for the abrogation of the Russian treaty showed that the link between the status of native and foreign Jews was growing clearer. Russia's very actions supplied the evidence, for restrictions on American Jews increased during the years in which the Russian government actively plotted the strangulation of its Jewish population. The obvious deduction on the interdependence of Jewish rights had been made even earlier, in 1881, by Secretary of State Blaine: "An amelioration of the treatment of American Israelites in Russia could only result from a decided betterment of the condition of the native Hebrew. . . . Any steps taken toward the relief of one would necessarily react in favor of the other.'' Jacob H. Schiff, a prime mover behind the abrogation campaign, openly spelled out the same principle in 1911:

> Our anxiety to see our Government take action should not be misunderstood. It is not because the Jewish people lay stress upon the admittance into Russia of a few hundred of their number who may annually wish to go there, but because of the conviction that the moment Russia is compelled to live up to its treaties and admit the foreign Jews into its dominions upon a basis of equality with other citizens of foreign countries, the Russian Government will not be able to maintain the pale of settlement against its own Jews.[41]

Seasoned by events of the half century between the Swiss and Russian affairs, American Jews in 1908 to 1911 were not consumed by the single passion to uphold their own status. They were aware of the successes that racial anti-Semitism had scored in Europe in the last quarter of the nineteenth century—in the enlightened West as well as the benighted East. In the United States they themselves were buffeted by a tide of social anti-Semitism which began to swell after the Civil War and showed little sign of abatement. Developments in both Europe and America had taught them that hatemongering and anti-Semitism could and did spread their poison from one country to another. They still believed that America was the best thing that had ever happened to the Jews, but they sensed that it too could not remain immune. Nineteenth century anti-Semitism had steered them to a more realistic view of their vulnerability and to the lapses that they might expect even from their government. No longer would they give vent to the same hurt feelings which their predecessors had displayed in the 1850s. In an increasingly business-like attitude, they established new organizations to cope with the ongoing problems of Jewish rights and acceptance in the United States and abroad. Slowly they were learning that self-interest, and not merely the noble sentiments of philanthropy, demanded that they defend their foreign brethren.

NOTES

1. *Occident* 16 (1858): 403.

2. *First Annual Report of the Executive Committee of the Board of Delegates of American Israelites* (New York, 1860), pp. 9–10; *Occident* 16 (1858): 346; and *Asmonean*, June 19, 1857.

3. *Occident* 16 (1858): 347.

4. See, for example, *Jewish Messenger*, August 16, 1872.

5. Reprinted in *American Foreign Policy: A Documentary Survey*, ed. Dorothy B. Goebel (New York, 1961), p. 25.

6. Thomas A. Bailey, *A Diplomatic History of the American People*, 9th ed. (Englewood Cliffs, N.J., 1974), pp. 167–68, 181, 268–72; and Oscar S. Straus, "Humanitarian Diplomacy of the United States," in *The American Spirit* (New York, 1913), pp. 19–38.

7. Joseph L. Blau and Salo W. Baron, eds., *The Jews of the United States, 1790–1840*, 3 vols. (New York and Philadelphia, 1963), 3:924–26.

8. Ibid,. pp. 927–29.

9. Ibid., pp. 930–52.

10. Cyrus Adler and Aaron M. Margalith, *With Firmness in the Right* (New York, 1946), p. 5.

11. Referring to prior instances of American humanitarian diplomacy, Aaron Moise of Charleston said: "That as they [the people of Charleston] had cheered the inhabitants of classic Greece, unfortunate, martyred, chivalric Poland in her struggles for freedom, that as they had hailed Texas in her resistance to tyranny, . . . they were now ready to raise their voices in behalf of wounded Israel." Blau and Baron, *Jews of the United States,* 3:947.

12. Ibid., pp. 934–37.

13. *New York Herald,* April 6, 1850. The paper also informed its readers that the manuscript record of the original trial, exposing the guilt of the Jews, had found its way to New York and was soon to be published. See also *Asmonean,* April 12, 1850.

14. Sol M. Stroock, "Switzerland and American Jews," reprinted in *The Jewish Experience in America,* ed. Abraham J. Karp, 5 vols. (New York and Waltham, Mass., 1969), 3:78.

15. Ibid., p. 79. Switzerland opposed the entry of the Alsatian Jews, a petit bourgeois class, convinced that they were usurers and swindlers.

16. *Asmonean,* January 24, 31, 1851. A brief biographical sketch of Waterman appears in Guido Kisch, "Two American Jewish Pioneers of New Haven," *Historia Judaica* 4 (1942).

17. Stroock, "Switzerland and American Jews," p. 79; and Morris U. Schappes, ed., *A Documentary History of the Jews in the United States,* 3d ed. (New York, 1971), p. 316.

18. Stroock, "Switzerland and American Jews," pp. 78–80; *Asmonean,* January 24, 31, February 7, 14, March 14, 1851; *Occident* 8 (1851): 613–15; and Schappes, *Documentary History,* pp. 317–18.

19. *Asmonean,* February 14, 1851, February 13, 1852.

20. Ibid., March 14, 1851.

21. Ibid., May 28, June 12, 18, 1852.

22. Stroock, "Switzerland and American Jews," pp. 83–91; and Schappes, *Documentary History,* p. 319.

23. Stroock, "Switzerland and American Jews," pp. 85–87, 93; Schappes, *Documentary History,* p. 321; *Occident* 12 (1854): 95–100; and *American Israelite,* June 30, 1904.

24. Stroock, "Switzerland and American Jews," pp. 94–96.

25. The facts for the remainder of this paragraph and the next three were culled from *Asmonean,* August 14, September 11, 18, 25, 1857; *Israelite,* July 31, August 21, 28, September 4, 11, 18, 25, 1857, June 11, 1858; and *Occident* 15 (1857): 291–96, 349–53, 423–35.

26. B'nai B'rith even appropriated $150 for studying the constitutional arguments. *Asmonean,* September 11, 1857.

27. *Occident* 15 (1857): 291–94; *Asmonean,* August 14, September 11, 1857; and *Jewish Messenger,* June 17, 1859.

28. *Israelite,* October 9, 1857; *Asmonean,* September 18, 1857; *Occident* 15 (1857): 296–97; and Stroock, "Switzerland and American Jews," p. 100.

29. Stroock, "Switzerland and American Jews," pp. 102–4.

30. *Dictionary of American Biography* 3:305–6; and *New York Times,* December 18, 1898.

31. Fay's dispatches to the State Department relating his activities appear in *Discriminations in Switzerland against Citizens of the United States of the Hebrew Persuasion,* 36 Cong., 1 Sess., House of Representatives Executive Documents no. 76, pp. 11–64, 74–75. The dispatches are summarized in Stroock, "Switzerland and American Jews," pp. 106–14, and are summarized with some reproductions in Adler and Margalith, *With Firmness in the Right,* pp. 306–19.

32. *Discriminations in Switzerland,* pp. 67–97.

33. Ibid., pp. 85–86.

34. Ibid., pp. 86–92.

35. Ibid., pp. 93–95.

36. Ibid., pp. 99–101; Adler and Margalith, *With Firmness in the Right,* pp. 321–22; and Stroock, "Switzerland and American Jews," pp. 114–16.

37. Stroock, "Switzerland and American Jews," pp. 113–14; *Discriminations in Switzerland,* p. 83; *American Israelite,* June 30, 1904; and *Occident* 18 (1860): 92–93. Although the Board of Delegates reported that the American treaty with Japan also singled out Christians for special protection, the text of that treaty, signed in 1858 and proclaimed in 1860, guaranteed Americans (without distinction) the free exercise of religion. Charles I. Bevans, comp., *Treaties and Other International Agreements of the United States of America, 1776–1949,* 13 vols. (Washington, D.C., 1968–1976), 6:670, 9:366.

38. Stroock, "Switzerland and American Jews," pp. 116, 118, 120–21; and Allan Tarshish, "The Board of Delegates of American Israelites (1859–1878)," reprinted in Karp, *The Jewish Experience,* 3:134–35.

39. Stroock, "Switzerland and American Jews," p. 81.

40. Naomi W. Cohen, "The Abrogation of the Russo-American Treaty of 1832," *Jewish Social Studies* 25 (1963): 3–41.

41. Ibid., pp. 3–4, 7–8.